THE REMBIS REPORT

ALSO BY MIKE REMBIS

Coffee

The Diary of Romeo Slim and the Cold White Room

THE REMBIS REPORT

An Observation

MIKE REMBIS

Mike Rembis

@Copyright, 2022, by Mike Rembis

All rights reserved. No part of this book may be reproduced in any form or by any electronic or mechanical means, including information storage and retrieval systems, without permission in writing by the publisher, except by a reviewer who may quote brief passages in a review.

Visit our website at MikeRembis.com

First Printing, 2022

For Marian and Ruperto,
may you meet in heaven

Contents

I
Stop Holding Your Breath — 1

II
Livingston — 6

III
Billings — 17

IV
Dogs and Ducks — 22

V
Great Falls — 28

VI
Forty-Two — 35

VII
Jeff's Neighbor — 40

VIII
Halloween in Livingston — 43

IX
Death of the Cassette Deck — 49

X Witnessing Stupidity	53
XI The Little Bighorn	62
XII Leap Year	68
XIII Arlo	74
XIV Dreams	79
XV Summer	86
XVI Seeds in the Wind	110
XVII Fort Benton	116
XVIII Time Travel	131
XIX Peru	136
XX Halloween in Billings	146
XXI Heroes	152
XXII Christmas	163

XXIII Another New Adventure	169
XXIV The End of the Road	179
XXV A Change of Scene	199
XXVI Life Goes On	203
XXVII Cannes	206
XXVIII Generosity	214
XXIX My Last Sale	223
XXX Politicalism	229
XXXI Austin	240
XXXII When Larry Met Mikey	245
XXXIII The Premonition	249
XXXIV Ruperto	255
XXXV Home	266

The Response File   272

Footnotes   345

Acknowledgements   347

FOREWORD

The Rembis Report began as a writing exercise to assist my mind in wandering so I could find ways to place my thoughts into words and to maintain contact with a multitude of friends when my wife Ellen and I ventured away from home. From spring of 2006 until 2009, for at least an hour a month, I dedicated myself to sitting down with an open mind to stare at a blank page until words were forced out of me that made some kind of sense. The prose became a series of emails that I sent with diligence every month to over 200 recipients.

Within many of the emails and replies you will find references to stage and screen work I have done, most notably, BEST; my TV pilot about a car rental on an island where nobody needs a car, and references to my Bestest friends, who helped produce the pilot episode. BEST, along with many of the short films discussed are available for viewing on the internet. Links to everything are maintained at mikerembis.com. References to other websites are included for archival purposes. Some that are now defunct may still be accessed through The Wayback Machine Internet Archive.

Immediately following some of my monthly emails are featured replies. Others may be found in The Response File at the end of The Rembis Report. Some grammatical and spelling errors, and exaggerated punctuations were left intact to maintain the personality and unique style of the senders.

Writing these essays on a regular basis helped me to find the many voices needed for my screenplays and to complete several other creative projects.

Along the way, I found a story to share.

I

Stop Holding Your Breath

Sent: Saturday, April 01, 2006 1:17 AM
Subject: The Rembis Report - Volume I

Okay, stop holding your breath.
    Here it is. The one and only Officially Sanctioned by me, Rembis Report. You may be asking yourself, "What is a Rembis Report?" Obviously, you have not heard the buzz, and that is understandable because there wasn't any. This is low-key, on the QT, whatever that means, for-your-eyes-only kind of stuff. The Rembis Report is designed to answer those questions you're all afraid to ask because I might keep talking out loud. Instead of a blog (that means weblog) which is a truly annoying form of correspondence because you have to search for it and log on with some password so marketing gurus can insert spyware into your computer and monitor your shopping habits, this is a newsletter, developed only for my dear and close friends who know me well enough to understand my liberal use of profanity. For your convenience, I am personally

forcing it into your email box whether you like it or not. How's that for service!

If you feel you may have received this correspondence in error, please hit reply and paste this into the subject line: I AM A LAME-O.

Then, come up with a good reason not to read the Rembis Report.

You know, something like this: Hi Mike, Please stop sending me crap. I am very boring and like my life the way it is and do not wish to be amused in any way. Especially by you. I prefer a dismal existence devoid of anything slightly interesting, informative, or entertaining. I would rather have snails crawling between my toes for something to do than to read your rambling philosophical prose and archaic wit. Please leave me alone and go away.

And if that's what you want - that's OK. I don't understand, but that's OK. This is just my way of keeping in touch with all of my favorite people. The plan at this moment is to send you this update once a month for the next 24 months. Now, don't think I'm getting lazy and won't answer your personal emails. I just won't answer the boring ones. Consider this whatever you like, online diary, nuisance, it's up to you.

So here's the latest. In case you haven't heard, Ellen and I are moving back to Montana next week. We came here to Florida 7 years ago this week and I must say, this has been an awesome vacation. Since moving to Tampa Bay we found pretty decent jobs and did a good deal of traveling. I got to make movies and commercials and be on stage and made many wonderful friends. I wrote a TV show. We adopted a dog. We bought our first house a few years ago. Today, we sold it. A brilliant sense of accomplishment swept over us as we took it all in.

Knowing that I am leaving in a week, I notice myself visibly moving slower. I've been looking a bit more closely at the way the sun drowns a palm tree when I walk by. I remember doing similar things in other places I have lived, Salt Lake City, Spokane, Baltimore. In those last days I remember specific things. Buildings. Stores. Once you know you're leaving, you look very closely at those things you want to take with you. Mostly it's just memories. I have a shell that I have been carrying around for 23 years. I have taken it on every long-distance trip I have ever been on. My shell has been to Venezuela, Puerto Rico, China, the Canadian Rockies, New England, etc. etc. etc., even L.A. I don't know how old it is, but when I found it on Vero Beach when I was 18, I instantly decided that this was something I would have for the rest of my life. I would take it everywhere! Oddly, it has become my obsession. I am looking at it right now and for some reason it gives me a sense of calm and security. I would be lost without my shell. And I don't know why. It's purpose, in a sense, is a lot like this newsletter. Suddenly, I need it. Writing to you and telling you what I am doing, reaching out to people I may never see again, and just want to hold on to. But unlike my shell, I can't physically take you with me, so this is as close as I can get to that sensation.

One person I and no one else will see again is my good neighbor Tommy Davis. He was my next-door neighbor and he died yesterday. 54 years old. Stroke. You would have trouble finding a kinder and gentler person than Tommy. He always had good things to say. Never complained. His concerns and opinions were well thought and balanced. He will be missed.

So quickly life changes. In 3 days Tommy will be buried and movers will be loading our belongings onto a truck bound for a 2,200-mile journey. We will load up our three cats and dog and go. And the new chapter begins.

I have already contacted 2 agents in Montana for acting representation and am getting there just in time for the summer acting work that may come to the state. We bought a nice little place in Livingston. No home phone yet, we move in on the 12th of April.

I am doing what I can to promote BEST. I have entered it into 3 pending film festivals, the Fort Lauderdale International FF, The 1st annual Sunscreen FF in St. Petersburg FL, and the Village International FF in Lisbon Portugal. I'll get feedback later this month for Sunscreen, next month for Portugal, and not until October for Ft. Lauderdale. Feedback is letting me know if BEST has been accepted as a competitor. The Newport Beach CA FF rejected us earlier this month. I am also entering short screenplays into Film Festival competitions where the top prize for screenplays is PRODUCTION! A short I wrote entitled, In The Moment has been entered in the Gimme Credit and FirstGlance competitions. The second episode of BEST, BLONDZILLA has been entered in the Boston International competition.

As for BEST, the concept, I am still soliciting agents for representation and will keep you updated on that as well.

So I hope all this answers some questions or creates some confusion. Either way it gets you to think. I'll check in next month after I've had a while to absorb life in a place where the chances of having a grizzly bear in your yard are pretty good (in Libby MT, we counted 13 grizzlies at one time!) and there is no daytime speed limit so I can drive as fast as I want.

Remember, that's what life is all about. Wild animals lurking outside your door and driving as fast as you want. Or something along those lines. I mean, what's life without a little danger? Where's the fun in that?

Yours Truly,
Mike Rembis

From The Response File
Volume I

Received: Monday, April 03, 2006 10:53 AM
Hi Mike,

Well, that time has come that you have been waiting so patiently. I admire your trust and faith which pushes you forward into the unknown and the positive attitude that you maintain even with the pitfalls of life. In many ways the silence and peace of Montana contrasted with the hustle and bustle of this area must be greatly appealing. As I previously mentioned, the mere name Montana has always had a positive impact on me.

I like the title of your short work entitled "In The Moment". With your dedication and fortitude the odds are greatly in your favor for "Discovery".

Thanks for sharing your talents with us in Picnic. You already know how much the audience enjoyed Howard. Several laughs in an otherwise serious play.

Take Care and may this be the beginning of all good things for you and your wife. Have a safe trip!

MK
GBY
Mary Kay Smith

II

Livingston

Sent: Monday, May 01, 2006 1:06 AM
Subject: The Rembis Report - Volume II

No, you didn't miss 9 chapters. We are using Roman numerals. If the Super Bowl can use them, so can I.

Apparently, some time while I was gone, Montana reinstated the interstate speed limit not to exceed 75, but so far, I have not been approached for exceeding that limit. My good friend, fellow actor, Chris Pio (stage name: Christian David) was not so lucky. Chris was good enough to step in at the last moment, the day we were leaving Florida and drive my car all the way here for me. The auto transporter I contracted never called me at all to pick up the car until we were somewhere in Tennessee, braving hailstorms, and tornadoes. That was on Saturday morning, when they were already a day late. "Hi, Mr. Rembis. I think we can have somebody out to pick up your car on Monday." I sent the caller packing on his miserable way after a well-deserved verbal lashing.

Chris drove a day behind us without incident until he reached Wyoming and was pulled over in a school zone. 27 in a 15. The deputy ran the plates and told Chris the car belonged to somebody else, not Mike Rembis. This must have stupefied and confused the deputy severely because she did not know what to do. "Do I call for back-up?" The car wasn't reported stolen, but the plates didn't check out either. "Are they forged? What to do? What to do?" In cases like this in small Wyoming towns a verbal warning is apparently good enough for the offense of confounding an officer of the law. Once I was in possession of my car again, and Chris told me about the incident, I checked my registration. I do indeed own my car.

I want to say THANKS once again, to Chris for saving me the hassle of driving two cars across the country. I've tried driving two cars at once before, and it's really hard, because you can't reach the pedals on both of them at the same time.

Our mixed breed motley canine, Mama Dog, did not enjoy the trip. She was fine until we crossed the Mississippi. At that point, she must have instinctively known she was so far from Puerto Rico that she may never taste a greasy fried tortilla again. From St. Louis to Livingston, she panted. It was quite disgusting. There was drool. Not pretty. But she's fine now. The cats handled the trip very well. There were no incidents, no messes to clean. They gave up asking "Are we there yet?" by the time we hit Georgia.

All in all, it was a nice excursion across the USA. Of course, most of you are familiar with Florida and the Eastern US. You don't start hitting vast stretches of interstate devoid of townships until you reach Iowa. From there and into South Dakota it is a sea of grass and willowy velvet alfalfa sprouting all around you. Then, you reach Wyoming and crossing into that state the sign welcomes you with a rodeo cowboy on a bucking bronco which is the silhouette logo they emblazon on the license plates. It immediately feels Western.

Suddenly, there are indeed cowboys riding horses and herding cattle. We drive past a huge black hole in the ground where they are harvesting the purest darkest coal you could ever see. You don't realize how huge it is until you spy down inside and see what looks like a Tonka truck at the bottom and the man standing beside is merely a speck.

Then, Montana. Once we pass Custer Battlefield, we skirt the Yellowstone River for the last 150 miles to Livingston. Each curve in the road yields a view that makes you wonder why you ever left.

But soon enough, you meet some of the locals and you remember. Montana in many ways still feels like the 1970's, smaller towns even bask in the hazy glow of the 1950's. It's an odd feeling. Ellen opened an account at the local credit union. A few days later, when making a withdrawal, the young teller was embarrassed to ask for identification because she never met her and she knows all of the customers at the bank. So apparently, if you're the spitting image of anybody around here you might be able to empty their account. Just go in drunk. That way you create an alibi. "How should we know why? It's your money. Stop making withdrawals while you're wasted."

My testament to the small town atmosphere happened when I went into a dry cleaners and they asked for my phone number. I didn't find this to be unusual, since they were going to type it into the computer and print me a ticket, but here's something you don't hear every day. "You're not in our system already? Sorry. We're not taking new customers. We just can't handle more business." WHAT? Are they out of hangers? Are they not in business to make a profit? I didn't even discuss how long it would take to get my shirts back. I didn't have a chance. I was dumbfounded.

So now I am doing my own laundry. At least I like to iron. It's something I'm really good at.

On the acting front, I have been accepted by Jules Model and Talent in Missoula and the other two agents in the state are looking at my headshot to decide if I look like somebody else they represent. I'm not really worried about that since I'm not from the inbred local stock. I got a very encouraging phone call yesterday. My cell phone rang and they asked to speak to me. My hackles went up instantly and I was on the defensive when I heard a strange voice. INTRUDER ALERT! INTRUDER ALERT! Obviously, this person is going to attempt to sell me something. Excellent! Let the games begin! "Who's calling?" I commanded. "This is Gary from the Boston International Film Festival." SHIELDS DOWN! SMILE, DAMMIT, SMILE! They don't call the losers! I lost all composure instantly. "That's me. Mike, me. I'm Mike!" Gary was just calling to let me know they are postponing decision making in my category for two more weeks. But that elation, when you think something good is about to happen, is just about as good as something good happening. I was thrilled to get that phone call.

I'm probably going to get the same rush when I find a dry cleaner to take my clothes.

So that's it for now. I leave you with these photos. Both are extreme examples of what it really feels like out here.

Take Care,
Mike Rembis

Exhibit A
Whereabouts Unknown

Exhibit B
Livingston, Montana

From The Response File
Volume II

Some replies were simply direct.

Received: Monday, May 1, 2006 9:35 AM
Maybe I'll move there and open a dry cleaners.......LM

While some were sent just to share a bit of happiness.

Received: Friday, May 5, 2006 10:29 AM
Fwd: The Hippopotamus and the Tortoise
I thought you'd all be touched by this. You never know where the next wave of life will lead.
Blessings! Priscilla

Forwarded from Trish Dempsey:

Tsunami-Orphaned Hippo Adopted by 100-Year Old Tortoise
NAIROBI (AFP) - A baby hippopotamus that survived the tsunami waves on the Kenyan coast has formed a strong bond with a giant male century-old tortoise, in an animal facility in the port city of Mombassa, officials said.

The hippopotamus, nicknamed Owen and weighing about 300 kilograms (650 pounds), was swept down Sabaki River into the Indian Ocean, then forced back to shore when tsunami waves struck the Kenyan coast on December 26, before wildlife rangers rescued him.

"It is incredible. A-less-than-a-year-old hippo has adopted a male tortoise, about a century old, and the tortoise seems to be very happy with being a 'mother'," ecologist Paula Kahumbu, who is in charge of Lafarge Park, told AFP.

"After it was swept and lost its mother, the hippo was traumatized. It had to look for something to be a surrogate mother. Fortunately, it landed on the tortoise and established a strong bond. They swim, eat and sleep together," the ecologist added. "The hippo follows the tortoise exactly the way it follows its mother. If somebody approaches the tortoise, the hippo becomes aggressive, as if protecting its biological mother," Kahumbu added.

"The hippo is a young baby, he was left at a very tender age and by nature, hippos are social animals that like to stay with their mothers for four years," he explained.[1]

This is a real story that shows me that our differences don't matter much when we need the comfort of another. We could all learn a lesson from these two creatures of God, look beyond the differences and find a way to walk the path together.

Trish Dempsey

"Life may not be the party we expected but, while we are here we might as well dance!" - Author Unknown

Or for self-promotion, which the Rembis Report was all about.

Received: Wednesday, May 10, 2006 1:06 PM
Subject: My future is in your hands!!!
Hi everyone,

How is my future in your hands? Well, I entered a singer/songwriter contest online (American Idol Underground) and my song started climbing up the charts pretty quickly without me telling any of my friends. I am 2 places away from being in the top 10; which would move me to the final round!

If you could take a few minutes to relax and listen to my song (for at least 1 minute, so your vote will count) and then vote, then I could very likely be pushed to within the top 10...because of YOU!!!

The procedure is easy. If you print this page with the explanation, you can easily follow it. And for all of my high achieving friends, if you pass this along to anyone else whom you think might enjoy the song so they can vote, that would be awesome!

By the way, my name is tcyla in the contest...I explain below...
Many blessings, and much thanks!
Priscilla Dubas (tcyla)

Why tcyla?

Well, when I signed up for this contest I didn't know how valid it was and who would be accessing what, so I created a fictitious name (actually, it's the name my sisters and I gave our pet turtle that my dad found in the middle of the road in the middle of the night...we came up with the name by taking a letter from each of our names—although it must have originally been spelled "tcila" so my sister Heidi would have a letter represented, but then it changed over time to tcyla...Note: this naming procedure must have been my idea because I have the most letters represented).

Then in this crazy contest, my song started climbing higher on the chart so I asked if I could change my name to my real name so people would really know who I am and I got no response from the company. So, who knows, maybe I'll be famous, but no one will really know who I am...hmmm...I'll really be hiding in a shell? Perhaps a prophetic name I chose to use?

Enjoy !

tcyla (priscilla)

III

Billings

Sent: Thursday, June 01, 2006 2:14 AM
Subject: Rembis Report Volume III

Tonight, I dined at The Rex in Billings Montana. The Rex is a 100+ year old establishment that has served generations of Montanans. It escaped the wrecking ball by only one day back in the 1970's when someone stepped in to restore it. It has beautiful brick walls and ornate woodwork and high vaulted ceilings with intricate square molding reminiscent of some of the old buildings in Ybor City. They claim that infamous personalities like Calamity Jane and Buffalo Bill Cody frequented the bar and ate there. As I stood at the solid marble urinal that has stood for more than a century, I couldn't help but wonder if Buffalo Bill peed here.

 Dining was indeed a pleasure, the lamb and potatoes exquisitely prepared with rosemary and garlic. Across from me sat a couple. They were probably in their 40's. The man wore his hair long, like a rock star, it flowed out below his cowboy hat. His date, his wife

I believe, wore a sparkling blue dress. It was unusual attire for a Wednesday evening. Certainly this was a rare and special occasion. A bottle of wine was ordered and a toast soon ensued. The couple looked rough. Like ranch people who worked 19 hours a day and only smiled when they heard bad news for somebody else that worked in their favor. The woman, I have no doubt, could kick anyone's ass. She was lean and sturdy. If she wasn't wearing a dress, you might call her "sir". I wouldn't call them an odd couple, they seemed to fit together. I never make it a point to eavesdrop, and in fact, I try to avoid it because I really don't care what anyone else is saying. But I promise I was not eavesdropping when the toast was made and they both said "I love you." And that was a lovely thing to witness.

I myself had an equivalent moment when I looked down at my appointment book today and found "I Love You" scribbled in the margin by my dear sweet wife Ellen. It's a very powerful sentiment. Even if Ellen was drunk when she wrote it and might not remember, it means a lot. So, whether you're drunk or not, please tell someone you love them. It's important.

I am very happy to report that my script BLONDZILLA is a finalist in the Boston International Film Festival Screenplay to Production contest. Please keep your fingers crossed for me. And toes if you can do that. There are 29 finalists and four prizes. Blondzilla is in the short narrative fiction category. Winners will be announced on June 15, 2006.

I also want to let you know about my epic poem COFFEE that has been transformed into a play by Robert DeWitt and Karl Bush. Coffee opens July 28 at the Tarpon Springs Cultural Center. I will not be able to make it, and I don't know what it's going to be like exactly, so for those who can, please attend a performance and report back to me with your reviews. Robert and Karl, if you could record it and send me a copy, that would be great.

At this time I would also like to say "Thank You" to Tom Thompson and Tony Armer for finally getting me placed on the Internet Movie Database with Waste of Space. Playing Jon Buhmed was a really fun role and I am told that it came across well on film. Even Stephen Soderbergh and Robert Redford left me out of the lineups for The Punisher, Oceans 11, and A River Runs Through It. It's good to know who your friends are!

If you follow the links to Darla Delgado you'll see the kind of buzz they are stirring up about one of the stars of the film and one of my BESTest friends. Also, there's an article/interview with Darla in the very first issue of Florida Film Monthly! Way to go Darla! You ROCK!

Have you heard about American Idol Underground?

Go there and in the Artist Search Box (left side) Type in "tcyla". This is Priscilla Dubas' moniker and she needs your vote. Take a minute and listen to her sing and I'm sure you'll vote favorably.

Finally, this month, I want to run an idea past all of you and I need your feedback. Once there was a movie called WESTWORLD that starred Yul Brynner as a psychotic gunslinger robot that goes haywire. Once I got out here to Montana, knowing what I know about actors and how they like to work cheap, I thought to myself, "Hey, why not start a Western-style theme park?" Of course we won't have berserk robots shooting the guests, but here's the whole shebang: During summer months, because the winters are harsh here, guests can visit an old west town and step right into the 1860's / 1870's. You arrive by stagecoach and check into your hotel. There are, of course, no cars, only horses and buggies. The 30 or so people that bring the town to life are all actors. For the guests 3 - 4 day stay, they witness, not just the old west way of life, but a drama unfold. A true western, where the bad guys start taking over town and the good guys ride in and by Saturday afternoon, there's a good old fashioned shootout, complete with special effects and dangerous stunts, and obviously compelling dialogue.

"I'll spit on your grave!"

"I'll piss on yours!" he replies and shoots him!

Then everybody celebrates at the barn dance that night and goes home the next day. I think this is the next step in live entertainment and I want to know what you think. Every single aspect of the guests' visits would be scripted with light improv as though they were really living in that time period. What do you think? Good summer job for an actor. How much would you pay as a guest? Remember, it's live theater 24/7. This is a luxury vacation.

So that's it.

I hope you've enjoyed hearing from me as much as I enjoy keeping in touch with you.

From The Response File
Volume III

Received: Thursday, June 1, 2006 3:46 AM

well mike it seems that you have alot of time on your hands to write us these lovely reports on all of our favorite subject, you! I got your call but than lost your new number, so if you call me again I WILL ANSWER. LA is well, LA. Thats all that can be said about it. At the moment I've been sleeping on my friends floor or at my newly aquired girlfriends house (I'm actually more like her boy-toy). If you want to know more about the trouble and excitement that I have gracefully walked into out here you must pay 99 cents for the first 10 minutes than 1.29 a minute.

xoxoxoxoxo,
Christian David

IV

Dogs and Ducks

Sent: Saturday, July 01, 2006 2:59 AM
Subject: The Rembis Report - Volume IV

No. It means four, not intravenous.
    Here we are again in the wee hours of the morning clattering away at the keyboard to bring you news from the Big Sky Country of Montana. One thoughtful and friendly reader who has enjoyed these tidbits has remarked that I must have a lot of time on my hands that I have so much to say, but the truth is I am very busy indeed. I just type fast. I only spend an hour or so on the R.R. because I don't want it to be long winded. Editing is kept to a minimum, so basically what I deliver to you is a rough first draft with spelling errors corrected to the best of my ability.
    I know what you're thinking - "When does the fun start, Mike? When?" Okay. Here it is. Today I saw a skunk on the side of a dirt road. It wasn't dead. It was very much alive, and it was a baby, so it was very cute. Speaking of cute, and wildlife, in Billings yesterday,

I saw an Exodus of ducks (the technical term is Duxodus) crossing the road and stopping four lanes of traffic. There were at least 50 of them. I don't know where they had to get to but they were headed toward Outback Steakhouse. Of course not one person dared to run over the ducks. Those drivers on the front lines held firm and helped to reinforce everyone's faith in humanity. I was not one of those drivers, and if I had been I would have stalled traffic as well, but sometimes, when I see ducks, I admit, I think about something fried up nice and crisp with orange sauce.

This makes me think about our trip to China a few years ago. (Vegans, avert your eyes). Ellen and I, in our quest for Peking Duck, found a nice little place down the street from our hotel. A true Chinese restaurant (in China) has a fantastic waitstaff of four to six people who all have a different function in serving you. One only brings tea. Another, only utensils and plates. Nobody brings napkins, however. For some reason, they just don't use them. One young lady, who I can only describe as kitten-like, delighted in scooping my food from the serving dish onto my plate for me after almost every third of fourth bite. We had ordered duck, but what we got was not at all poultry. It was a tangy seasoned meat, served with native vegetables and rice, noodles, soup, even spring rolls, but no bird. So halfway through the meal, although it wasn't duck, it was supremely delicious, and authentic a meal as any other we had on that trip. So we decided to inquire about what we were eating. Nobody in the restaurant could formulate a sentence in English and our Cantonese was non-existent. So when they heard us speak they heard "dug" which apparently translated to "dog". I don't know the breed.

You see a lot of dogs sitting in vehicles in Montana, more so than in other places. Rarely do they bark at passers by. They wait for their owners to return from stores or offices that are being briefly visited.

Our dog, Mama, named for her sagging nipples and puppies when we found her in Puerto Rico, and whose exact breed also remains a mystery, has taken to riding around town and sitting in the car. She knows we might be going out for dog food. Dogs are well adjusted and accepted members of society here. They walk around small towns freely, like ducks going from pond to pond. In Gardiner MT, there were a few different "town dogs" who strolled in and out of the bars. There was a yellow lab who carried around a 2 x 4 everywhere he went, and a Malamute named Niki that would stay at our apartment sometimes in the winter when it was cold. Then Niki would go out and hang around town somewhere else the next morning. When I drive through small towns here, I still see dogs wandering about. It's nice to see that some things have not changed.

On the self-promotion front, Blondzilla did not win in Boston, but I have entered my short script, In The Moment into two more script to production contests. I will keep you updated on that. I did get a positive response to one of my queries for my TV show, BEST. A production company in LA requested my top two scripts, so I sent them Blondzilla and Behold The Power Of Cheese.

I had one audition a few weeks ago for a role in a feature film that is going to be filmed here next month. I haven't heard that I am not going to be cast, so, always optimistic, I expect that I will. The movie is A Plumm Summer, which is based on the true story of the kidnapping of Froggy-Doo, a puppet that was stolen from a local TV personality here in Montana 40 years ago. This just in from the screenwriter: "He's not a puppet! He's a marionette!"

I'd like to take a moment and direct everybody to the Myspace page for Counter Intelligence where you can watch a short produced by my good friends Scott Reus and Tom Thompson and also featuring one of my BESTest friends, Georgia Chris. It's good fun for everyone.

That is about all for now, so I will leave you with these photos of actual nature in the wild. Elk and Bison in Yellowstone and a Magpie on my front lawn.

Take Care, Mike

Exhibit C
Bison and Elk

Exhibit D
Magpie

V

Great Falls

Sent: Monday, July 31, 2006 10:11 PM
Subject: The Rembis Report - Volume V

It is disappointing that there are people who don't like to drive. Maybe they don't have the right car, or they drive in the wrong places, or they listen to radio programs that frustrate them. I have heard people talk about the fastest route, the shortest way, the best time of day to avoid traffic. For some reason they seem to be missing the point that getting there is half the fun.

I love to drive. Being behind the wheel at the helm of my ship steering across the asphalt ocean is about as much freedom as anyone can ask for. The level of joy reaches its peak when you are driving along a desolate highway, rounding beautifully sculpted curves at very high speeds and there is nobody beside you, clutching your dashboard with their nails digging in and screaming "We are going to DIE!" That's the best.

I have found a new road that I love to drive. Highway 89 from

Livingston to Great Falls. Go ahead, get out the maps. This is one of my new favorite American Highways. Some of my others include paved backroads of the Palouse region of Washington State, south of Spokane, Utah Highway 95 from Hanksville to Fry Canyon, and the Blue Ridge Parkway near Cherokee North Carolina. This stretch of Highway 89 starts in the Shields Valley between the Crazy and Bridger Mountain ranges. Going north, the Absarokees fade in your rear view mirror as you pass miles of sagebrush and blink through the cowboy towns of Clyde Park and Wilsall.

At the Meagher County line there is some road construction that has progressed nicely over the last month that I have been driving up here. In another two weeks it should be paved. That is what every driver lives for, fresh pavement. Smooth. Clean. Inviting. The road work ends by the time you reach Ringling, another lost burg just south of the junction with Highway 12.

White Sulphur Springs, just up ahead marks the near halfway point of the journey. Here you can have your gas pumped and your windshield cleaned for the same price you would do it yourself. I always stop to take advantage of this. Then the plains and sagebrush are left behind for pungent pine forests, deep and green. The road is shadowy in the early morning and your senses and reactions perk up with every furlong. Sometimes there are deer standing beside the road, or ground squirrels, or birds. An affection for sobriety at the wheel is evident. The pathway is constantly scanned for any hint of movement, because if there is one thing out of place that you are not ready for it may kill you. The road winds over Kings Hill past the ski area where there is a 200 foot drop that awaits one who is less than alert. There are skid marks on one particular corner, the first one that warns you to slow down to 45, where they disappear over the edge and into the forest. That blaze of tire tread is enough to remind you to take the signs seriously.

Over the hill sits the tiny lumberjack's hamlet of Neihart. There is nothing going on there. There is one bar/motel/restaurant/gas station where they don't pump your gas for you and a convenience store with almost nothing for sale called The Son Of Man Project. The owner there is collecting donations so that he can buy Big Baldy Mountain and place a mansion on top dedicated to Jesus Christ.

"Then what?" you ask.

"I'll live up there." he answers. Believe it or not, he's serious. So, obviously, you've had enough of Neihart.

Back in the car. Up ahead in Monarch the road zips through a rocky canyon and jumps out into the wheat fields. This morning I drove alongside a pronghorn antelope who was dashing along about a hundred yards from the road. I slowed down and clocked him at about 47 MPH. In another twenty miles, you see the sign for Malmstrom Air Force Base and Great Falls appear before you. At 10th Ave SW and 49th Street you drive through the first traffic signal in 187 miles. And you have only seen six towns.

Each of these towns, large and small, all have distinct personalities. They are indeed very much like islands separated by vast landscapes and connected only by a sliver of pavement. None are, of course, as cosmopolitan as Manhattan or ethnically diverse as Miami Beach but they are nonetheless unique. Some have a cash machine and some don't. In most places the ethnic diversity ranges from Irish to Nordic heritage and that's about it.

Great Falls is intending to enter the 21st century sometime later this decade. In this part of the country they know you're not from here because not only haven't they seen you before, they confirm it by reading your license plate and pointing it out to you. It is obvious that I am from another county. Visitors from other states and Canada draw greater attention and require even more scrutiny. They might be trying to use some different money or something. I wouldn't have wanted to live here back when they changed the $10 and $20 bills, I am sure that threw them all out of whack.

Exhibit E
Advertising in Great Falls, Montana

Selling advertising in Montana I have noticed a great deal more people rejecting the internet products I have to offer. In Florida, they made the decision based on internet usage vs. print media. Here, I hear things like, "I don't want my phone number on the internet. You don't know what kind of people are going to call you."

"Do you know what kind of people are going to call you when they pick up a phone book?"

"Normal people who don't need a computer."

So that's the kind of business to business relationships I am developing here. The simple TV commercials and basic billboards that you see here are evidence that the pricey marketing gurus have yet to exploit this market.

On to more important things. I took a hike in the woods where there was a lot of horse manure on the trail. Unfortunately, this attracted a lot of flies. There was one fly buzzing around in front of me that was so big it could have worn a name tag. I could just picture him with Eddie Murphy's voice; "Hey, how you doing? Welcome to the forest. You're our first visitor today. Boy, it's a hot one today, isn't it? Why don't you take your shirt off, let your skin breathe? There you go. Don't that feel better? 'Hey, Everybody! - Breakfast!' What's that? He tastes like nachos? Well, save me some. Okay, no pushing, there's plenty for everyone. Hey! What do you think you're doing? Don't go swinging your shirt around like that! You could hurt somebody! Lookout now! We got a crazy one here, dangerous when they get like that! There he goes! Now he's running. Go for the eyes! The eyes! That's right, inside the glasses!"

So I don't think I'll be hiking there again this summer.

All is quiet on the acting and writing front. I did get another hopeful call, this time from a talent manager in Los Angeles who would like to read both BEST and COFFEE, so I sent him copies. We had a long discussion about career goals and seemed to click, I'll talk to him again in another week. I haven't heard any reviews of COFFEE, The Play yet, so somebody, please go see it and give me an unbiased report.

In the meantime, enjoy your drive to work. I know I will.

Mike Rembis

VI

Forty-Two

Sent: Friday, September 01, 2006 1:00 PM
Subject: The Rembis Report - Volume VI

The smoke is not too bad today in Livingston Montana. On Wednesday, the interstate was closed for a 75 mile stretch because the wildfires had jumped the highway. The Derby fire, so named because it started in the vicinity of Derby mountain, is currently reported to be 156,000 acres. When it was first sparked by lightning a few days ago it had quickly spread to 42,000 acres, so it has basically quadrupled in size. Houses have burned and bridges have been lost, but the good news is that the annual Reed Point Sheep Drive has not been cancelled for this Sunday and we will be in attendance.

When I first heard that the fire was 42,000 acres, I winced, because the number 42 has always held ominous connotations for me. When I had been robbed, once as a child on my paper route, the amount lost was $42. I reported this to Willie Pope's parents, and they offered in return one of his Christmas presents right out from under the tree. I had rejected the toy and insisted on cash, which I am not sure to this day whether or not I got my money back. I know that Willie wasn't very happy with me because I not only reported the theft to his parents, but I maced him as well. I am also hoping that Willie is letting bygones be bygones because he just got off parole.

Another time I was robbed when hitchhiking in Central Florida and I lost my glasses and $3.42. I walked around blind for two weeks while I waited for a new pair to be built. That was in 1983 before the technology existed to build glasses in a few hours.

When a duo of robbers held up the bank in Pixley on Green Acres and took Arnold Ziffel's $5 dollar bill, the robbers holed up at the Douglas farmhouse and tried to take Lisa's diamond ring, which was insured for $42,000.

In the play Picnic, a character I was cast as last year, Howard Bevans, laments to his beloved Rosemary when making observations of his life and his unwillingness to change, "Rosemary, I'm a 42-year-old man!"

In Douglas Adams' epic novel The Hitchhiker's Guide to the Galaxy it is discovered by the greatest minds in the universe that after years of pondering the question "What is the answer to everything?" The answer is indeed, 42. This has in fact been studied extensively by mathematical theorists and physicists who cannot get that number out of their heads. Here are some of the facts they have uncovered:

There are 42 dots on a pair of dice.

It takes 42 days for an ostrich egg to hatch.

The average diameter of a one-carat diamond is 6.42 mm.

There are more than 7,000 varieties of apples grown in the world. The apples from one tree can fill 20 boxes every year. Each box weighs an average 42 pounds.

In the 1820s, the average American consumed 10 pounds of sugar a year. Today we eat about 420 pounds per year, the equivalent of eating six candy bars a day.

There are 42 year-round research stations in Antarctica.

In 1935, the police in Atlantic City, New Jersey, arrested 42 men on the beach. They were cracking down on topless bathing suits worn by men.

According to the Data Group, grandparents spend an average of $42 per grandchild for a birthday gift.

It takes 17 facial muscles to smile but 42 to frown.

Not many people have heard of a glass harmonica, because there are only about 30 people in the world who can play it. It was invented in 1761 by Benjamin Franklin and is made of up to 42 separate hand-blown glass bowls placed on a rotating spindle that the player rubs with his or her fingers.

Elvis Presley died on August 16, 1977. He was only 42 years old.

Rosa Parks started the boycott of the Montgomery, Alabama, buses in 1955 at the age of 42.

The seventh planet from the Sun, Uranus, is tipped on its side so that at any moment one pole is pointed at the Sun. The polar regions are warmer than the equator. At the poles, a day lasts for 42 Earth years, followed by an equally long night.

A standard 747 Jumbo Jet has 420 seats.

The youngest person to take the position of U.S. president was Theodore Roosevelt. He was 42 at his inauguration. Next youngest was John F. Kennedy, who was 43.

In the United States and France, a septillion is represented by the number 1 followed by 24 zeros; in Great Britain and Germany, it is the number 1 followed by 42 zeroes.

Why all the hubbub about the number 42? Well, tomorrow Keanu Reeves and I both turn 42. Some interesting facts about Keanu and I. We are both:

Allegedly actors.

Americans born on US Army Bases in foreign countries. Me, Bremerhaven Germany. Keanu, Beirut Lebanon.

Extremely handsome and debonair.

So what now? What happens when you become 42? We shall see.

My dear BESTest friend Jill Ginter was recently cast in an upcoming episode of Boston Legal, so look for her in an episode entitled "Fine Young Cannibals."

I heard great reviews about Coffee, The Play, so I am very pleased about that. Robert DeWitt put on an extravaganza for the eyes and ears and not to be outdone, is still developing Coffee for an even bigger production, and shopping it to major markets. Stay Tuned…

I myself have been cast as The Barber in "Man of La Mancha" at the Firehouse 5 Playhouse, here in Livingston MT. As long as the fires don't get too close, the playhouse won't live up to its name and the show will go on. I'm going to play it safe and lie about my age.

Take Care,

Mike Rembis

From The Response File
Volume VI

Received: Thursday, September 7, 2006 8:49 AM

Mike;

You are a remarkable person! Look at all the friends you have! And look at all your talents! God Bless you. And by the way - I was in the first National Tour of "Man of La Mancha" with Richard Kiley, Jose Ferrer, John Raitt, and one more - I can't remember right now. It lasted for three years. I understudied and performed the role of Sancho many times. I did Sancho in about 6 other productions of Dinner Theatre, Summer Stock, etc. And I've directed it. I love it. All the best to you.

Take care, and God Bless again,

Victor R. Helou

Oh! Take a look at a website I have - screenlegends.com

VII

Jeff's Neighbor

Sent: Sunday, October 01, 2006 1:45 PM
Subject: The Rembis Report - Volume VII

This month I had the considerable pleasure of reciting my poem COFFEE on the radio here in Bozeman on KGLT. They called for poets and I responded. I shared the vocal stage with a few others who paid a visit to the studio that day. The first fellow who stepped up to the microphone can be properly described in one word: creepy. Before the show, when he introduced himself to me, he made a point of telling me that he used to live across the street from Jeffrey Dahmer and witnessed the cavalcade of policemen, coroners wagons and news media that paid so close attention to the gruesome events at hand and shined the tiny spotlight of infamy on his crude little neighborhood in Milwaukee Wisconsin over 15 years ago. I suppose that he suspects most people would find that fascinating.

I myself witnessed history once. Sadly, I saw the Challenger explode into a puff of smoke and drift back down to earth in a flurry of sparks, while everyone else saw it on TV. I however, do not use this tragedy as an icebreaker.

The Creepy Man, whose name I did not commit to memory, was, I swear, the spitting image of Jon Voight. At first glance I thought it was Jon Voight, and I believe most others would make the same assumption at first glance assuming you know what Jon Voight looks like. For those who don't know, Jon Voight is indeed the father of Angelina Jolie who surprisingly looks nothing like him. But I digress, back to Creepy Man.

Creepy Man was the first to recite among the ten poets who were scheduled. I have no idea what his poem was about. It made absolutely no sense at all and he felt the need to break into his own ramblings to explain them, which he did incoherently. To make sure that I was truly paying attention and had not just been prejudicially bored at the aspect of listening to another poet, I quizzed others who also listened to the show for their armchair view of Creepy Man and the votes were unanimous. I was right. He made absolutely no sense to anyone. All I can really tell you was that somewhere in the body of his text he mentioned Quantum Physics which most people can't understand anyway. For all we know he was explaining a very realistic advanced theory of time travel through light propulsion that was supposed to rhyme (but didn't) and is the smartest person on Earth. The moderator assured me that she would be screening future applicants a bit more closely.

The play I am now in, Man of La Mancha, opened on Friday night and runs for three more weeks at the Firehouse 5 Playhouse. It's a cute little production that truly defines what community theater is all about; almost anybody can get a role. What surprises me most is that the director also plays the role of the Duke/Prosecutor/Knight of Mirrors. (Yes, that is the same role, 3 characters in one). I must confess, the entire story confused me from the very beginning because I wasn't sure why Alonso Quijana kept slipping in and out of his fantasy world of Don Quixote, but after a month of rehearsal and being forcibly committed to memory, I realized that basically, it's all about the music.

The main plot (the tale of Cervantes) is thin and simple. The fantasy world of his characters Quijana/Quixote and the Manservant/Sancho Panza are a vehicle for the music. After a month of rehearsal, this soundtrack is the only music I know. It permeates my brain and I involuntarily keep hearing, not only the songs I sing as the Barber, but the entire production. This much rehearsal creates an internal music shuffle that also includes snippets of dialogue. I don't even think about my lines before I walk on stage, as I have in the past, they just happen. I have become a robotic singing actor that delivers everything on cue.

The one thing I am sincerely fighting is internalizing this so much that it absorbs me into the confusing state that Dale Wasserman must have been in when he wrote it and created the concept of a play within a play. Because if that were to happen, and I understood it better, I might wind up like Creepy Man, striving to explain my writing to you, and then having it make no sense at all.

Maybe Creepy Man is the Man of La Mancha.

VIII

Halloween in Livingston

Sent: Thursday, November 02, 2006 1:43 AM
Subject: The Rembis Report - Volume VIII

It was about 6 degrees this morning. Fahrenheit. Not Celsius. Not particularly fun on the first day of November let alone any day of the year when you are not used to it. Winter comes right after summer in Montana. There is no fall. Certainly, there are trees changing color and dropping leaves, but it does not happen in a leisurely flow that is evident in the thermometer slowly dropping in digits day after day. No. Not in Southwest Montana. Not this season anyway. This year it was like a car crash. Sudden. Frightening. Jarring. A few weeks ago it was 75 degrees and then the next day it was 20. It stayed that way for almost two weeks and then zipped back up to 70 again. Overnight, we went from parkas to t-shirts. So it stayed that way for another week and two days before Halloween the wind blasted through and it dropped down to 20 again, this time with a few inches of snow.

When you move to a climate like this from Central Florida it is difficult to adjust. You wonder, who exactly is in charge of the weather here? Why are we skipping Autumn?

Of course, Montanans who have experienced this before are unfazed by it. Sure, it's a little cold, but look at the bright side; no hurricanes. I suppose that would be a redeeming factor. We live up on a hill here in Livingston and while there are no true hurricanes we do get bursts of wind that must top 80 - 100 MPH. I am not exaggerating. Our house shakes during the windstorms that may come unexpectedly day or night. It actually feels as if the roof is going to be ripped off or we may be tumbled from the foundation.

Last night, on Halloween, we were disappointed to have not one trick-or-treater arrive at our door. I did not expect to have absolutely zero, but that is what happened. So, to make the most of the holiday and enjoy some costumed revelers, we drove down the hill to a more residential neighborhood and walked about where houses were decorated in tombstones and mummies and cobwebs and such. There were plenty of people dressed for the occasion, brandishing flashlights, or Jedi lightsabers and although there was a waxing moon hanging over the valley it was still quite dark because there just are not very many streetlights in this town. It was also a dangerous trek because there were sheets of ice under the blanket of leaves that buried the sidewalk. Ellen fell once, but without incident, she is okay. When we drove back to our hill, it appeared extremely dark and that's when I realized our nearest streetlight is over a block away. You can see a lot of stars from up here.

The sights you see in the sky in Montana are spectacular at times. Last week, when I was driving up Highway US 89 to Great Falls, I was just approaching the town of Ringling (by the way, they finished paving the road on that stretch and it's awesome!) and over the mountains I saw a flash in the sky, like an explosion. It was about 7:10am and not yet light out. I don't know what it was, but when I told people about it we surmised that it must have been either a meteorite or a lost hunter firing an emergency flare. If it was a hunter, he is probably frozen to death because if I was the only person who saw the flare, I did not report it to any civil authorities.

On my way back from Great falls I drove through Lewistown and south on Highway US 191 through Harlowton. On that stretch of road you get to experience one of the greatest wind farms in the country. There are dozens, perhaps hundreds of windmills in every direction. They are massive structures about 200 feet tall with 100 foot blades that command you stare and take notice. I parked for a moment and watched, and wished I had a camera.

Many times I am carrying a camera and this month would like to share with you some of the sights I have witnessed in the big sky.

On the acting and writing scene, Man of La Mancha ended without incident. We had a few sold out shows and it was a fun production. My queries for BEST brought me a significant prospect the other day. A production company requested three more scripts for consideration and asked me how I was being represented. I immediately got on the phone with a manager I had begun a rapport with in September and explained my situation. He has agreed to work with me. For now, I am keeping both the manager and production company anonymous because all agreements, other than a signed release are pending and no ink yet exists. The manager is based in Beverly Hills and handles over 30 talents. The production company was responsible for bringing a successful reality show to ABC last year. So please keep your fingers crossed and let's see what happens.

Hopefully, I won't get lost and freeze to death while I am waiting for one of these guys to call me back, because I don't plan on having a flare gun with me. But I did get new batteries for the camera today. At least I'll be able to take a picture.

Exhibit F
A rainbow over a wheat field near Great Falls

Exhibit G
The plume of smoke coming from the Jungle Fire as it consumed acres of forest only 10 miles from my front porch in Livingston, Montana

Exhibit H
Sunset as the camera battery died - Great Falls, Montana

IX

Death of the Cassette Deck

Sent: Friday, December 01, 2006 9:17 AM
Subject: The Rembis Report - Volume IX

When you are not using your own computer, the internet can be an unruly beast. This month I am writing from the warmth and safety of my in-laws home on Staten Island, far from the frozen tundra of Montana. When we left it was below zero and there is no doubt that our pets fear that we may never return and that we are human popsicles stuck to the ground out there somewhere, but of course, they will have no problem partaking of the kindness (food and water) that our devoted pet-sitter brings daily.

We are fine, safe, and warm in the mild climes of the Greater New York area. We are here to celebrate my mother-in-laws 80th birthday and reunite with those who have not seen us in many months. One thing I notice in all of my journeys are things that change and those that do not. In the almost two decades I have come to visit Staten Island, I notice very little change. In this house in particular, the only major change I can truly make note of is the computer whose keyboard I am typing on now. Up until about five years ago, it wasn't here. But on every occasion I have visited, I recall it requiring some sort of maintenance. Most people who have been using computers for a while understand the need for basic maintenance as a car needs an oil change. For those who a computer is a relatively new appliance however, the thought of basic maintenance, deleting cookies and defragging, are non-existent. So, when I appear and perform these basic tasks, and the results bring about remarkably better and faster performance, I am honored as a computer guru, which I am not, but I gladly take the bow because, let's face it - I'm the one who did the long overdue oil change. But does that make the ISP let you log on the dial-up server any faster? Short answer: no. So, I am saving this correspondence as a word document right now and you will have it whenever you got it. Get it?

    I saw a commercial today and realized that I have been watching technology die right before my very eyes. A few weeks ago I was riding with a coworker in my car and she asked me how old the car was. "Six years old." I said. "Why?"

    "I just didn't think they made tape decks any more." was her answer.

    Did they stop? Apparently, they have! I just learned this in the last few weeks. How un-hip is that? Is this what happens when you turn 42? Sure I've got a CD player in the car and a DVD player at home, but I still haven't sprung for the I-Pod or the Ti-Vo and I still haven't ditched my VCR. How would I watch Twin Peaks without it? Every once in a while I think about the 8-Track player my dad had in our Ford LTD Station Wagon. It worked great. We had Tony Bennett, Berlioz, the Star Wars and Close Encounters soundtracks and life was good. You never had to rewind. (Actually, you couldn't.) Now these things are gone. I am sure if I looked on eBay right now (if Verizon would let me on the internet) that I could buy an

8-Track player and all the tapes I wanted. I remember my favorite of all - Pablo Cruise. You probably can't get that on a CD. Maybe you can, I don't know.

The TV commercial that spurned this train of thought was a little girl showing her grandfather an MP3 player and him asking what it was. Then he showed her an old radio and she asked the same thing. In my lifetime I have witnessed the birth and death of the 8-track, the cassette, and the VCR. Is new technology really that good, or is it just a conspiracy to make you upgrade? As long as there are resale stores and pawn shops where I can buy tapes, I won't give up my cassette player unless you can pry it out of my cold dead fingers! Of course, I doubt that with all the technology out there and the legendary success of Pablo Cruise that anyone will want my tape deck, but that's not the point. I was horrified when one of my tapes skipped and I realized that I needed to clean the heads. Most of you know what I'm talking about, but for those younger folks in the audience, a head cleaner is - (stop laughing, it's not dirty!) well, actually, it's made for something dirty, but not like you think. A head cleaner eliminates dust and grime from the tape decks receptors (heads). And here is the point, as long and drawn out as it is - I don't have a head cleaner anymore and I can't find a place to buy one! Ain't that a kick in the head! It makes me wonder what would happen if my tape player or VCR actually broke. Would there be anyone around who could fix it? I can only imagine some old hippie living in a garage somewhere looking through a crack in the door to the alley asking "What You need fixed?"

"Tape deck. It ate my Best of Arlo Guthrie."

"Sounds serious. Who sent you?"

"Guy at the Disc Exchange, said you could help."

"Maybe I can. Maybe I can't. Either way, it's gonna cost you."

And anyone who owns cassette tapes can appreciate how invaluable they truly are. Just like an old album with all of the posters and stickers they came with and the words to the songs on the inserts, when you listen to your tapes they are more than just music, they are your music. How could you live without that?

As far as music and the internet goes, there are plenty of things to listen to, thousands of choices awaiting discovery, on TV, hundreds of channels, and always something new to watch. So you ask, what about BEST? Short answer: Hang on! I have a good feeling about this. I think I told you about the producer who wanted to read more and the manager who said he would represent me. Well, there's nothing in ink yet, but nobody has told me "NO", so as far as I'm concerned I consider that good. I'd like to direct everyone to my page on MySpace which is my little slice of internet heaven that I have been developing over the last few months. There is a 9 minute intro to BEST that was edited by our good friend Jeff Crabtree who wrote our theme song, Share My Banana. Thanks Jeff. And if you would like to read my latest full length screenplay please log onto TriggerStreet and search for GREAT FALLS. It is the story of a teen that is plagued by tragedy when he threatens to reveal a secret. Give it a few days, I don't think I'll be able to post it until later next week, but if I can get it up earlier (once again, not dirty!) I will. You see what the internet does to people's language? That would never happen with a tape.

I'm going to listen to my Richard Pryor album now. So, until next year - Happy**************Holidays*******!!

Okay, maybe with some tapes.

X

Witnessing Stupidity

Sent: Monday, January 01, 2007 6:53 PM
Subject: The Rembis Report - Volume X

How many times do I have to explain this? It means 10. Ten. It's not rated X. Anybody can view it.

But how many can understand it? That's the real question, is it not? Welcome to 2007. For some it came as a roar, for others a whisper. Some people woke up alone, some with their lifelong companions, some with nearly complete strangers at their side and others in jail cells. For those fortunate to awake today, they began what we call The New Year. Some are breaking resolutions or holding off until tomorrow to begin some life changing regimen. My New Year's resolution is to keep being myself. I wouldn't want to be any other way. I actually like the way I am. Very comfortable with my own phobias and quirks that may disturb or annoy other people mainly for one very simple reason: because those phobias and quirks may very well disturb and annoy other people and annoying people is what I do best.

Every late December the media looks back at the year and rates or compares it to other years. Sometimes there are benchmarks, as this year was recorded as the warmest year on record by meteorologists. Other indices record stock markets or box office ticket sales or births and deaths. Every type of every thing is recorded. If you want to find out anything about an annual record you need not look farther than the internet and you will get the most up to date results available. Something our media does every year is to place things on a list. Many times it's a Top Ten list. Few do it as regularly as David Letterman but who is choosing what goes on these lists is purely limited by what information they have to begin with. We all have access to the same information, yet when it comes down to deciding what is the most extreme or entertaining in non numerical fashion (where you can't count clicks or views or dollars, for instance) that trivial list is decided upon by only a few media producers locked in a room together simply trying to decide what trends people will talk about on January 2 so that they tune in next year. Countdown lists may include fashion faux paws, what are now called Bush-isms, and the most beautiful women on the planet.

It is difficult to read these lists and agree with any judgements made unless you were only exposed to the same information as the reviewer. So, of course, each of us must make up his/her own Top 10 Most Whatever Lists. We all have an opinion about everything so deciding what belongs on our own personal lists is only important to ourselves and once we establish these lists, we rarely change them, and this form of selfishness becomes one of the most beautiful examples of freedom in the world. You can make your own list.

I am constantly finding myself rearranging the only list I keep. I don't write it down every day or move the numbers up and down with magnets on a dry erase board because sometimes it changes fifteen times in a day and I myself am confused about what belongs at the top. By now you know me well enough that you realize I can only be talking about one thing. The Stupidity List. It changes constantly and I am always amazed when I have to move something to the number one slot because it seems to happen quite frequently. Because of the mercurial nature of the list, I can not truly give you a Top Ten for 2006. I have given you highlights over the past several months, dry cleaning and car washing being at the top of my list for the service industry out here in Montana because it is simply done wrong here. I'd like to add snow removal as well now that I think about it. One incident that rose to the top and stayed there all day happened a few weeks ago when I went to a coffee place in the mall that had a big neon sign exclaiming "Espresso" and had an espresso machine directly across the counter. I figured with that much information at my disposal, it wouldn't be unreasonable to ask for a coffee with a shot of espresso, something I order from other shops regularly. The man said to me "What do you want?"

I thought he didn't hear me. "A coffee with a shot of espresso, please."

But he did and he yelled at me "I don't do espresso!"

"You sell espresso, don't you?"

"I told you! I don't do espresso!"

And I left without any beverage at all.

This psychotic behavior is more common than you may imagine out here. Another day I had to put something at the top of the list was when I was walking Mama Dog in the hilly fields behind our house and found something stupid. These hills are public lands that are regularly utilized by dirt bikers to slosh around on muddy days or just have fun going up and down steep grades over 45 degrees on warm dry days. When I got to the extreme Northeast corner of the property I found an abandoned truck stuck in the mud. It was a four wheel drive Chevy Crew Cab with Wyoming plates. The driver and occupants apparently used poor judgement when deciding which track to take and were bogged down to the framework. There were boards and blankets and ropes which were ripped to shreds trying to heave the two ton vehicle out of the mud to no avail. There was no sign of alcohol but there were about 40 empty Red Bull cans in the back which makes me suspect that the occupants were younger and more daring. They obviously had to leave to get help to get the truck out. Of course, upon exhumation of the vehicle and the ride home they would draw the one obvious conclusion about driving through mud pits. "Next time, we need a bigger truck."

The next time I went walking there, about a week later, the truck was gone. In the distance I could hear the rev of a motor and thought there must be a dirt biker headed my way. Then I spied on the hill above me a truck about a half mile away. Was it the truck? It was fighting to go uphill at about a 60 degree angle. I don't walk over there when it's wet because I know how steep it is. So here was this truck, going uphill, stuck. Gears grinding, mud flailing, tires burning rubber on the rocks and roots below. It would go about ten feet and slip back five. I thought the guy was going to topple over and I would watch him roll down to the bottom and have yet another episode in my life where I get to call 911. But he slipped and scurried all the way up the hill and about ten minutes later he made it to the top. I don't know if it was really ten minutes, but it felt like it. I wasn't going to go and help push him uphill, that was for sure, but felt it was my duty to watch him crash and report it to the proper authorities if necessary. If that happened I might even get my name in the paper. So there he was, cresting the hill and was safely on his way home when - No. It can't be! That stupid idiot shot right to the top of my list when he turned around and drove straight downhill in a fresh patch of snow and started doing donuts sideways on the mountain.

As I walked away I could see him in the distance cresting the hill and going back down, tempting death or at least bodily injury over and over again all for the joy of doing something that made him feel free. Even if he did hit the top of my list, that hill may have made the top of his at the same time.

So whatever your lists may be comprised of I hope you have a safe and Happy New Year and don't wind up like this.

Take care,
Mike Rembis

Exhibit I
Highway US 89, south of Niehart, Montana

From The Response File
Volume X

Received: Tuesday, January 2, 2007 12:18 PM

Happy New Year Mike! Wishing you all the best and great success in 2007.

I do have some sad news however. My dear friend, Priscilla Dubas, (Aunt Martha in Arsenic and Old Lace) was killed in a car accident and died on Christmas Day. I'm sure you remember what a lovely person she was and how she brightened everyone's day. Below is an article from the St. Pete Times regarding her death. I will miss her beautiful spirit.

Trish Dempsey

Teacher loved music, singing
The St. Petersburg Times
By ABHI RAGHUNATHAN and CASEY CORA
Dec 27, 2006

Priscilla Dubas spent her life saturated in music. Her father was a composer, record producer, guitarist, and singer. Her husband is a music teacher and conductor. And Dubas, 47, spent 20 years teaching music and giving vocal lessons, most recently working part time at Gibbs High while she pursued her own singing career.

In the aftermath of her death Christmas morning from injuries suffered in a car wreck on Friday, her family and friends recalled that love of music. "Her passion for singing was there since she was little," said Elicia Ruilova, 40, Dubas' cousin and a Tampa resident. "Singing was her."

Dubas was leaving the Tyrone Square Mall on Friday night after purchasing etiquette books as a last-minute gift for one of her two sons. She turned her Toyota Camry left onto Tyrone Boulevard and into the path of an oncoming 1989 Jeep Wrangler driven by Corbin Milligan, St. Petersburg police said. The Jeep's front stuck the driver-side door of her Camry.

Milligan was not seriously injured. Police say no charges are pending. Dubas, who appeared to be wearing a seat belt, was taken to Bayfront Medical Center. She hung on through the first 24 hours, but then her condition suddenly worsened, Ruilova said. She died Monday morning.

This holiday season Dubas' entire family - many of whom live in the bay area - planned to gather at her grandmother's house in south Tampa. Instead, they gathered at Bayfront, praying Dubas would recover. So many friends and relatives came, Ruilova said, that hospital staff found a room for them.

Before she died, Dubas was concerned about the driver of the Jeep and wanted to make sure he wasn't hurt, Ruilova said.

Dubas was a fixture among local music students for years. George Caram, 15, remembered her as a tough but fair teacher. "She wanted the best from us," said Caram, a clarinet player.

In addition to teaching dozens of students, including several years on Gibbs High's full-time faculty, she sang professionally and recently produced a CD titled Lover, Come Into My Garden. She could play a variety of instruments and sang in at least five languages, but especially loved jazz.

She was also very involved at Indian Rocks Baptist Church and recently sang and acted in a church musical called A New Heart for Christmas.

Andre Dubas, Priscilla's husband, conducts youth orchestra at the Pinellas County Center for the Arts at Gibbs High. They have two sons, Ryan, 20, and Brandon, 18.[2]

XI

The Little Bighorn

Sent: Thursday, February 01, 2007 7:41 PM
Subject: The Rembis Report - Volume XI

Still can't believe you're actually reading this every month, can you? Just like I can't believe I am still witnessing people answering cell phones in libraries and seeing librarians do nothing about it. Here they would be rightfully justified in dishing out public humiliation and they don't take advantage of it. I think that is just sad. If you can publicly humiliate a total stranger in exercise of some sort of actual authority, you should. That's the American way.

Here we are again, facing a second full month of winter. It is ice cold here in Billings. We had a brief and violent blizzard this morning that dropped two inches of powder on the city and then quickly exhausted itself into a clear blue sky. The radio reported that the interstate was closed for about 50 miles from Wyola to Sheridan. I just drove there two days ago. The road was clear and snow glistened on the hills under the nearly full moon. Dazzling stars blinked on the horizon. Even with the almost 1,000,000 candlepower of our lonely satellite you could still see them shining from light years away. If you have never experienced the solitude and briskness of a frigid winter night under an unclouded sky where not one human light can be seen, the answer is simple - You need to.

It is this kind of quiet that lets you hear your own heart beat. This level of twilight that brings your imagination into focus. The retracting mercury and the bitter air stinging your cheeks reminds you that if your car does not start this far from other people that it is going to be a very long night because your cell phone is definitely out of range. Even coyotes are not howling. Happily, I keep my vehicle in supreme running condition, so it started. Driving along moments later, I am tempted to punch off the headlights and rocket into the night on that ribbon of black between the snowbanks, and I do, but only for a blinding second. Two seconds would have been two seconds too long. It is not something I condone or recommend, but thrilling just the same.

As I drove down that stretch of interstate that knifes through the center of the Crow Indian Reservation I passed Custer's Last Stand at the Little Bighorn River and at the next exit in Crow Agency noted the latest achievement of our generation - The Little Bighorn Indian Casino. No kidding. It truly exists. I didn't stop for a closer look at either the battlefield (I have been there before) or the casino. To me, a battlefield is simply a graveyard and a casino is simply a casino. Now the scalping is monetary instead of a bloody nature. Not that there's anything wrong with that. The gleaming neon and flashing LCD display seems to send the message that if you set foot on this land you run the risk of some sort of loss, but you are certainly welcome to do so because you'll probably have fun in the process.

In the territory of Montana, however, a casino is not a big deal.

Anyplace that has 2 or more gaming machines qualifies as a casino. The maximum number of gaming machines allowed is 20 per establishment. Those rules may not apply to the reservation, I am not sure. There seem to be over 100 casinos in Billings alone. They are everywhere. Grand Avenue is a thoroughfare of one gaming palace after another, each more sorry than the next. They are not majestic hotels towering to the sky with brilliant architecture and pleasing facades. They are dumps. Remodeled Taco Bells or abandoned Pizza Huts that now serve as refuge to the addicted gambler. I have no idea how many there are in the entire state, but it appears to be an epidemic. Word on the street is that each one of these places nets at least $60,000 a week each. Trust me, this is not a gambling Mecca. There are no dice games, no roulette wheels, and only rarely found upscale places offer a poker table, and usually only on Saturday nights with a $20 buy-in and maximum $5 pots. There is no blackjack. No baccarat. No wheel of fortune. People do not come here to gamble, but these places do prosper.

In my job selling advertising, I regularly walk door to door, cold calling each establishment in a city block and it is inevitable that I walk into the warm smoky casinos to find the proprietor, who will never be seen, and leave my number for a later call back, which is unlikely. But in each of these little dens of inequity you are almost always guaranteed to see at least 3 or 4 people huddled over their individual screens, much like those huddled over internet computers at the library, pushing buttons and adding to the coffers of some unknown casino owner, nickels, dimes and quarters that add up to thousands in the hopes that they have chosen wisely the right digitally-dealt cards or keno numbers to exact a payoff that will bring them fortune. The highest any of these machines can pay out is $800 according to Montana law.

As I see more of these places, now even in the remote belly

of the Crow Agency, I am reminded of my childhood at the racetracks of Detroit. I was raised to gamble. I love the track. The musk of horses and mud and the rainbow of losing tickets that littered the ground is still a fond memory for me. Visiting tracks on rare occasions in more recent years, that fantastic thrill has faded away with the distance of my youth. Gambling, I know, is not what the track was supposed to be about. It was the Sport of Kings, for only the master of a kingdom could afford to enjoy such noble beasts for peasant entertainment. And we peasants would stand at the side of the homestretch shouting at the thundering hooves racing toward us, edging each other with flaring nostrils and sweaty backs to be the first across the line. That was the thrill of the track.

Some time in the last twenty years, that was somehow forgotten to some extent. The multitude of colorful tickets were replaced by singular bland playing slips that all look alike and create a sea of pink scrap paper. There is only one Las Vegas. I have not been there since 1984, but I do see it's triumph being touted on TV regularly, so I know that it is of superior value when it comes to gambling as a form of entertainment. I am sure there are other places like Monte Carlo or some Caribbean paradise that hold their own as well.

But what is it that is truly being accomplished in these little leftover buildings that have been transformed into gaming halls? Las Vegas is it's own industry. It feeds families and builds lives for an entire metropolitan structure and keeps many people employed. These so-called casinos only serve as a drug for the self-abusive that can't help their addictions, or so it seems.

There is no romance or great memories to be made in the Montana casinos, not that I can see. There is nothing sporting or Kingly about it. So the question is, what true purpose do they serve if not to promote public prosperity, basically jobs? Are they just a waste? Maybe. Or, maybe they are places people can go to privately lose money on that fantasy that they are a little closer to Las Vegas, in spirit, while not even realizing they are humiliating themselves in public.

It's hard to say.

BEST Update - I am pleased to introduce you all to film editor extraordinaire Marcos Baca of Great Falls. Marcos has created a beautiful 5 minute short which has been submitted to the latest reality show concept by Mark Burnett and Steven Spielberg, On The Lot, a competition for aspiring filmmakers like myself. It is not up for public viewing yet, but please check that site in a few weeks and look for BEST in the comedy section. Marcos is also working on a complete re-edit of the entire project that will be available in upcoming months. I'll keep you posted.

Please check out Get Butt Nekked. This is Jill Ginter's website promoting her lip treatments and cosmetics. Not only is Jill one of my BESTest friends, she also makes a fantastic lip balm (I recommend the Pumpkin Pie) that works great in the harsh cold Northern breezes and keeps my lips moist and kissable, just ask my wife.

Finally, this month we must say goodbye to another one of our BESTest friends, Priscilla Dubas. You may recall her from a previous R.R. when I told you about her performances to be heard on American Idol Underground. Please take a moment to enjoy one of her performances. Priscilla passed away last month in a car accident outside the Tyrone Square Mall in Pinellas County Florida. I will miss her a great deal because I loved hearing her responses to my communiques like this one. After R.R. IV, she wrote this:

Dear Mike,

Your writing style in this email has that Garrison Keillor sort of tender, down home, quaint, warm-fuzzy feel to it. You might consider creating a radio show or even compiling your writings, like this one, into a book...Your e-mail letters are not the typical "read and run" type e-mails. I actually had a few minutes, so when I saw your email I went and made my cup of coffee, so I could take my time, sip my coffee, and sit and enjoy reading.

Thanks for sharing...

Priscilla

I do not take your responses for granted, and if you were not important to me, you wouldn't be on my list.

Take Care, Drive Safe, and Play for fun when you visit the casinos.

Mike Rembis

XII

Leap Year

Sent: Thursday, March 01, 2007 11:39 PM
Subject: The Rembis Report - Volume XII

February. Gone in a flash. Four short weeks without any extra days. Why is that? All the other months get 30 or 31, but not the redheaded stepchild of the Gregorian calendar. No, 28 days is all you get - 29 if you're good, but don't even count on that every year. I once rented a car to a man from Houma Louisiana whose birthday fell on Leap Day, February 29th. I remarked to him that he was the only person I had ever met with that birthday. He responded that he had only had seven birthdays his entire life. It sounded somewhat devastating but I am sure it makes that day even more special when it happens so rarely. You know, like total solar eclipses or parole, they're worth waiting for but never happen soon enough. I wonder if people remember his birthday more readily or forget it altogether.

    I sat and wondered what to tell you last night for quite a while.

I stared at the blank template on my screen and put tremendous thought into which keys to tap to convey this months' message. I knew not to rush it. You have heard the expressions "Haste makes waste." or "Slow and steady wins the race." I trust such heeding especially when trying to produce a quality product. But once a project begins - you finish it. Period. No matter how it comes out in the end you can say you achieved something. I never rush the creative thought process. In all my writing, even this, I just let it happen. But, when it does happen, that's when the true test of patience begins. When is a finished product a finished product? When do you stop tweaking? When does one stop rambling and get on to the next subject? Ahem...

Now, then. I am naturally impatient. I don't like to stand in line for anything. I'll do it, but I won't like it. I have even skipped lunch on several occasions because the line was too long. I have driven hundreds of extra miles because I couldn't stand to wait for an oil change. Same thing goes for a car wash. I am a prime example of I Want it NOW! This latest transition moving from Livingston to Billings was indeed a test of patience. Waiting for banks to process paperwork. Waiting for contractors to show up. Waiting for them to finish their work once on site. It seems like a never ending process. There's even one contractor who finished the job, but left all his tools behind and never charged us - not yet anyway. Maybe we'll get lucky and end up with free tools and no bill. So "Good things come to those who wait." may actually, in this case, ring true. Who said that? A great many thoughts on the subject of patience have been brought forth over the centuries. If I had a favorite it would probably be this one:

"You must first have a lot of patience to learn to have patience."[3]

There are tons of quotations out there, search the internet. You won't find all of them, but you get the idea. Will I ever learn to be patient? Is it something that can be learned? I think of patience as a plant that needs to be cultivated and whose soil needs to be turned constantly yet will still never fully develop to fruition. You can quote me on that.

This morning I checked Ellen's lottery ticket for her. She won. Not a lot, but enough to get a few more tickets for the next draw. Yet when I brought it to her attention, I was rebuffed for having checked it. She likes to check it herself, of course. I should have known better. I feel the same way about looking at the TV guide. I don't want anybody to tell me what's on. I have to see it for myself! Telling me just takes all the fun out of it. Ah! Impatient one.

I had a great deal of frustration recently that was all in my mind. I mean, where else could it be? I frustrated myself with my own impatience when I asked my good friend Marcos Baca to edit BEST into a 5 minute short for the On The Lot competition. I was like a little kid on a road trip asking as politely as I could in random emails "Is it done? Are we there yet?" Marcos, ever the stern taskmaster and perfectionist, with the steady hand of a ninja warrior would write back "Patience, Grasshopper." Well, not in those exact words, but that's what he meant. Before long, a short was produced, and I breathed a sigh of relief.

Then came the chore of uploading to the website. The upload took about an hour. I filled out every form of necessary paperwork and mailed it with the DVD and I waited.

And waited. And Waited. And WAITED. AND WAITED~! And Finally! Three short weeks later (which is how long they said it would take) BEST magically appeared for viewership. I also wrote to The Lot with a few humble emails asking "Did you get it? Are we there yet?" Of course the responses were prompt and courteous and as assuring as the adult driving the car. "Patience, Grasshopper."

I often hear people talk about TV shows or movies that tell a long somewhat sophisticated tale with many characters and plot twists being so involved that it's confusing so they don't like it. Two of my favorite current shows, Desperate Housewives and LOST (you see how that almost spells BEST, pretty cool, huh?), are regularly trounced upon as having so many story lines that viewers lose interest and stop tuning in.

I will not be one of them. I love those convoluted puzzles that keep you guessing. I suppose that is the one thing I do have patience for: A good story.

I hope that you enjoy the R.R. as much as I enjoy bringing it to you and will keep reading until the very last line, whenever that may be. Although there have only been twelve issues so far, this is just the beginning. You have got to see how it ends, don't you think? So if you can bear with me, just as the man from Houma waits for his next birthday (I'm sure he remembers every one), I promise you'll be glad you stuck around to see what happened.

By the way, April Fools Day will be the R.R.'s First Anniversary and the 13th issue.

Do the math on that one.

Please check out Homesick by my good friend Adam ArNali. You might even recognize one of our BESTest friends Georgia Chris in a quick cameo. Then take a peek at what some other Florida filmmakers have On The Lot.

Finally, please log on and enjoy five minutes of BEST. This clip features the acting talents of Annette Millan, Landon Price, Carl Hunter, Greg Jones, Tilisia Roberts and myself. Music by Jeff Crabtree of Dirty Crabber. Editing by Marcos Baca. And thanks again to the entire BEST crew who brought this piece to life.

Until next month, just hang in there.

If somebody can wait 4 years for another birthday, you can wait a month for the next chapter.

Patience, Grasshoppers.

From The Response File
Volume XII

Received: Monday, March 5, 2007 10:39 PM
Mike,
I can tell you exactly why February has only 28 days. Get a load of this.....

Many centuries ago during the Roman Empire, there were two leaders. Julius Caesar and Augustus Caesar. Both of whom had months named after them. July and August. Originally, July, August and February had 30 days. Augustus Caesar had so much of an ego, that he thought he should have the most calendar days. So he stole one from February and put it in his month. When Julius Caesar found this out, he got upset. He figured that if Augustus Caesar can get away with this, so can he. To this day, August and July have 31 days and February has 28. I could be wrong but I think February is the only month not named after a person so it ended up losing days.

D.D. (Dan Diaz)
My Reply:
WOW!
I did not know that. Cool. So my question now is - what does FEBRUARY mean?
Mike
Dan's Reply:

As best as I can figure, it's the name of either a Greek or Roman god. All the planets are named after Roman gods, so the months of the year that aren't named after Roman emperors were probably named after the gods themselves. For example, Sunday is called what it is because it's "the day of the sun." and Monday is "the day of the moon." I know that Juno is definitely a Roman deity which is where June came from. You may want to look it up in a library.

D.D.

F.Y.I.

According to The Old Farmer's Almanac, February comes from the Latin word februa, which means "to cleanse" and was named after the Roman holiday Februalia, a month-long celebration of purification and atonement that took place every winter.

XIII

Arlo

Sunday, April 01, 2007 3:39 PM
Subject: The Rembis Report - Volume XIII

For those of you daring enough to disregard the number 13 and open this email, you are in luck. This is the one year anniversary of The Rembis Report.

13 monthly issues packed into one year? But how? More importantly - Why? The answer to the first question is simple. I write a new report on the first day of every month and today, April Fools Day, April 1st is the 13th time I have written a report. So we are starting a whole new cycle and by this time next year you will be enjoying Volume 25. Got the math down? Good. Okay, now for the second question.

Why? Because I need to write. Thoughts do us no good if we don't share them. Those journals that people scribble and keep tucked away for shame or posterity or out of fear don't really serve any purpose. So what purpose am I endeavoring to pursue? To be plain and simple, I want to be famous. There, I said it. I want paparazzi from the National Enquirer following me around when I return stale donuts to Albertsons, which happens more than I'd like to admit.

I'd like to be known as a storyteller. The guy who has a good story to tell with lots of good segues, tangents and plot twists that all lead to the surprise ending and take you on a verbal roller coaster ride. One grand storyteller whom I have always admired was Samuel Clemens, AKA Mark Twain, whose more popular moniker I recently learned means Two Depths, after the way riverboat soundings were termed on the mighty Mississippi.

I have read not all, but several of his stories and in the absorption of those volumes always enjoyed the yarn for what it was, a big ball with a lot of thread to get through before you reach the end. Being trapped within the boundaries of a story somewhere in the middle is really what a story is all about. It is the essence of emotion that you have as you turn the page or watch the next scene or hear the next paragraph. On some occasions, people have stopped me in the middle of a story to tell me that I am long-winded and of course I can only counter by saying "You're right." and continuing on with the next chapter.

I have one friend who likes to tell stories and many times starts getting to the good part and then says "Long story short, what happened was . . . . " and I find it deeply disappointing because all I'm getting is a taste; the rind, the seeds, a little pulp and then all the juice in the middle goes down the drain. And that is what separates storytelling from gossip. If you don't get the juice and then relate the story to a third party, well, then you have to squeeze your own juice and who knows how the story will really end up. This is how bears become Bigfoot and reputations are destroyed.

Last night I was privileged once again to witness a near living legend, Arlo Guthrie, performing here in Billings at the Alberta Bair

Theater. I had not seen Arlo perform since 1993 in Spokane Washington. At that performance he told many long-winded stories, but not Alice's Restaurant Thanksgiving Day Massacree, explaining that "It's pretty long and that's why they make records and that if you've heard it before, well, then you know what happens. Besides, I sound the same in person as I do on the record anyway." After that show, Arlo sat on the edge of the stage and I waited my turn to walk up and greet him, shake hands, and tell him how important Alice's Restaurant was to me when I heard it once on the radio alone in my car on Thanksgiving Day a few years prior. It made me feel not so alone, especially since I had not been drafted.

Last night was a similar show to the one 14 years ago, his style remains unchanged. Arlo is confident and comfortable and long-winded and this time around shared stories of his tour to Australia, his version of Joseph and the Amazing Technicolor Dreamcoat, and finally, the long awaited, Alice's Restaurant. Of course, he was right all those years ago -He does sound the same as he does on the record. Nonetheless, it was a treat, and now I can say I've heard it "LIVE" and go to my grave with one more measure of completeness in my life. I didn't stick around after the show this time, that one personal exchange with Arlo was pleasurable and remains a fond memory, and not knowing if he would visit with fans after this show, I didn't want to set myself up for disappointment if he didn't.

What I enjoyed most about it is not how I felt about the concert afterward - I felt good, my ears weren't ringing, Arlo doesn't do that - it was the feeling I had in the moment of listening to the stories. Both the ones I had heard before, like Alice's Restaurant, which was recited perfectly, word for word, (that's verbatim, for you uppity types) and those that were new to me. Arlo's leisurely, rich lyrical Bob Dylan-esque voice keeps you engrossed and hanging on every syllable. At least it does for me. For those folks who like a story to end just to know what happened and tell others "Cut to the chase" this would never do.

As I was walking Mama Dog through our neighborhood this morning an old man pulled up next to me before he turned the corner and rolled down his window. I would have to say that I would guess his age to be somewhere close to 85. I believe he thought I was somebody else at first, thus prompting his jovial greeting.

"Good Morning!"

"Hi!" I replied cheerfully.

"What?" he responded, not hearing me. "Good Morning! I said."

"I know. I said Hi!"

"Okay! Hi!" he told me, and then added "Life's too short!" and he drove off.

Although the entire exchange took only a few moments and didn't make a lot of sense, that's exactly what happened. This is in stark contrast to a conversation I had with another man earlier in the week. He told me about a friend of his, a man who lived to be 93, and how sad he was to watch him deteriorate physically while still having such a sharp mind. He told me this, "I don't ever want to get that old. Boy, I hope I don't live much past seventy."

To me, that just doesn't make a lot of sense. It's like quitting a job. When it's not such a bad job, you hang in there until you get fired is the way I see it. Such is life. As long as I can feel a morsel of pain it means I am still alive and that far outweighs death. "Basically, I don't want to go. I want to live to be the oldest man in the world." I told him "I could be famous for it."

"Well, Mike, there's one thing you haven't considered that my old friend told me about. He had outlived most of his friends, now isn't that sad?"

Maybe for them, I thought. If that happens to me, I'll just keep making new friends, like the old guy who probably thought I was somebody else this morning who told me "Life's too short."

If that is really true, then I can never tell enough stories and like Scheherazade, the legendary Persian Queen who told the stories of 1001 Arabian Nights to stave off execution by her psychotic husband, it will be storytelling that keeps me alive. With luck, I will build a reputation like Arlo has and become legendary or follow in the footsteps of Mark Twain and become immortal.

My good friend Maureen Smithorbob, who I acted with in my last Florida stage production, Picnic, is now a published author herself. Congratulations, Maureen!

One of my BESTest friends, Darla Delgado, has been seen in a popular Bud Light commercial entitled Plotting Apes, filmed at Busch Gardens.

Please keep in touch and let me know what you've been up to so I can share your success story in the next R.R. Things are pretty quiet for me on the acting front, but tonight I will be auditioning for the only male role in FICTION by Steven Dietz at the Venture Theater in downtown Billings. Let's see if I can break a leg or two.

If it seems like an unsavory theater and I get any bad vibes, I'll just yell, "Life's too short." and walk out. Arlo would like that.

XIV

Dreams

Sent: Tuesday, May 01, 2007 3:44 AM
Subject: The Rembis Report - Volume XIV

The black man in the starched white shirt, who was sweeping the floor as I played the video poker said to me "You need to learn to trust your partner at band camp." So vivid was this image that when I awoke, I immediately wrote down what he said. I don't know what it means, but this is what happened in my dream.

Dream interpretation has been a pastime for thousands of years. It got Joseph out of jail and got him a good job working for the Pharaoh. But how do you interpret my dream? Why did this exact image bubble up from my psyche and how is it that I remember it so well? As if it really happened?

I can still remember a dream I had as a child. I told my mother about it right away. Nothing horrible, but something any child with a lot of Disney toys would have been susceptible to. I grew up across the street from one set of Grandparents and around the corner from the other. I was four or five, maybe even six, and in that dream I stood on the corner looking toward Grandma Brown's house. I couldn't see her house from there, it was the fourth from the corner, but what I could see was the three story apartment building on the corner. A massive red brick structure that once housed a corner store. I never knew anyone who lived there. It was kiddy corner from Ethel Kobylka's house on Kirkwood and Central. It was night in my dream and on the top of that building were giant plastic cartoon character statuettes and bright lights and fireworks. Biggest of all was a smiling Mickey Mouse head that seemed to rise above it all and float on a tether like a balloon. I stood watching. That's the whole dream and I still remember what it looked like as if I awoke from it yesterday.

I remember other dreams too. Once again, I have no idea why. Sometimes, they stay with me for years. Sometimes not, they fade away and I can remember the essence of what was dreamt, but not the actual dream itself. I remember a lot. People I have never met in real life, who come and go. Places, cities and forests and buildings that I revisit regularly, all built from my imagination, conceived for a purpose that I do not know. So it is haunting.

Does this happen to everyone? I think so. Dreams are not new. It has even been speculated that we are all the characters in the dreams that God has. If that is the case, God has been perpetually asleep.

One of the oddest incidents I ever experienced upon waking was recalling the dreams I had of a woman named Anna Coudriet. I never met her in real life. I remember what she looks like. She told me very good things. What those things were I can not remember now, for I dreamt about her nearly 20 years ago. The odd thing was that when my wife, Ellen, awoke, she reported speaking with the exact same woman, by name, whom she had never met in real life. When I search it on the internet now I find pages like Find A Grave and can't help but wonder why this very strange thing happened to us. Did we somehow, in fact speak to someone who once existed? If so, which one was she? And more importantly, why? And most frightening, how?

What happens when we are asleep and unable to control what happens to us? Children who sleep soundly often wet themselves. Adults who sleep soundly may not react to a fire alarm. It happens.

Sometimes there are waking dreams, when you think you see something and ignore it, because you are sure you must be dreaming, and if you ignore it, it will go away. One night in our Clearwater home, I awoke and thought I saw a head looking at me. It was peeking around the corner at me in the dimness of night. My glasses were off, so it was blurry, but it was there. I covered my head. Did I see something? I looked again. It was gone. Later, we learned that a cat-burglar had been targeting our neighborhood, thieving from women's purses and wallets left on nightstands while the occupants slept soundly. Did I see somebody? Or did I dream something?

Bridging the gap between reality and whatever you want to call it - the ether-world - the one thing that I always have left is the memory. Sometimes it is seared perfectly into my mind, like this one. I was playing a poker machine in a nice casino. I don't know if I was winning or losing, but it was clean. The black man wore a white shirt, cummerbund, dark slacks and walked with a broom and a dustpan with a long handle. He was not old, not a child either, but thin and smiling. His hair was cropped short. I would dare to call him African American, however, he could have been from Canada or France or someplace else that black people live that would eliminate the possibility of him being American in any way. I would guess, however, that he was definitely of African descent. It was as if he were offering me valuable advice that I should heed. "You need to learn to trust your partner at band camp." And that's everything I remember for sure. I also remember walking around the casino, playing different machines, and I think I saw a skee-ball arcade there too. At least, I feel like I did.

So what was he trying to tell me?

I have never been to band camp. Whatever the analogy is, I don't know yet. Using the term "learn to trust" denotes that I do not currently trust this partner, whoever it is. Making it a "need" tells me that this is an important message and I suppose that is why I can't get it out of my head.

In sales, we utilize the word "need" daily when relating our product to our clients. It builds desire. So what desire is the man with the broom and dustpan referring to? Your interpretations are welcome.

I sometimes wonder, and I think others wonder this too, if dreams are real, if there is another place we go when we sleep, where we have another, more fantastic life than the one we wake up to? Like in A Nightmare On Elm Street. You can't help but wonder that when dreams are so real. I actually ponder what will happen when I go to these places and meet these people again, if I do go and meet them again, since it is seemingly something I have no control over. Sometimes when I am awake, living the life of Mike Rembis, I wonder if it is a dream, but that is a rare sensation.

I went to a restaurant in Columbus Montana last week for a bite, and nothing on that menu appealed to me. I sat down. The waitress brought water. I read the menu and left. That was somewhat dreamlike. I was almost a character, a chapter in the life of that restaurant that never happened, that the author decided to cut and rewrite. Whoever the author of my life is sent me down the road and I wound up at the McDonalds drive through. Despite the warnings that I recently absorbed from the movie SuperSize Me and the conflicted feelings I had about eating meat after watching Fast Food

Nation I found myself trapped between my hunger and the minimal dining choices to be had in Columbus. There are a handful of cafes and a Subway. My own personal taste steered me, quite literally into McDonalds. For those who don't know, it's not true Irish fare. There is no haggis or cabbage or spotted dick and the Shamrock Shakes are not really made with shamrocks. So you know.

When I rolled down the window to place my order at the drive through, parked a mere thirty yards away were two semi tractor trailers hauling livestock. Incessant mooing wailed through the air and the girl at the other end of the speaker could not hear me well. The cattle bellowed over and over a sad, scared, and lonely howl. You could almost hear them saying "Nooooooooooooooooo! Noooooooooo!" as if to pull me out of line to unlatch the doors of the trucks and set them free.

That was a defining and surreal moment. Knowing that these poor animals have one purpose in life that is not their own. They are most certainly on their way to slaughter or to be fattened for later use. What if I just hit the gas and left? Take that McDonalds! Would it accomplish anything? Not really, I would still be hungry, they would still be doomed, and the meat that was already on the grill would simply be sold to the next customer. I paused, wondering how I could change the world before I said "Big Mac Combo, Supersize it."

"$5.55 at the first window." she said. The cattle protested further. No! There's still time! Try something else! Chicken! Fish! Celery! I looked over at them and could only see little snouts pushing through the grates of the trailer. I tried not to make eye contact. I ordered fries and a Coke. On the radio, a story came on about how Coca-Cola is sponsoring the Olympic torch as it is carried across Asia for the next Olympics. The image that immediately flashed into my mind at that moment was one of a candlelight vigil at Virginia Tech for slain students a few days before. I am certain, or at least I hope it was unintentional, but thousands of those candles were being held in place by wax paper Coca-Cola cups.

A lot goes through your mind in only a few moments. Did the cattle really know what was going down right before their eyes? Did they understand what was happening to them and where they were going? Were the bovine rumors true? I hoped that the cattle wouldn't get my license number as I drove away and put a hit out on me. I mean, it's not personal, it's business. I would hope they would understand that.

So I drove away with great respect for the hoofed beasts, and refusing to let their sacrifice be in vain, honored their spirit and consumed every bite of those two all beef patties special sauce lettuce cheese pickles onions on a sesame seed bun.

Maybe Shakespeare said it best as Hamlet:

"To die,--to sleep;--
To sleep! perchance to dream:--ay, there's the rub;
For in that sleep of death what dreams may come,
When we have shuffled off this mortal coil,
Must give us pause: there's the respect
That makes calamity of so long life."[4]

With such short lives and so much to ponder, what do you suppose cattle dream about?

Please take a look at what my friends have been up to. This just in from Darla Delgado: "See me as the Picture-Taking Girl in the Bud Light Super Bowl Commercial "Plotting Apes" (USA Todays #7) and a new video by Adam ArNali on his website.

As for me, I just finished the first draft of a screenplay I have been collaborating on with my good friend Dave Barrett. No, you can't see the screenplay, it's hush-hush, very top secret and on the

QT. When we make the movie, we'll let you know. Don't call us, we'll call you.

Unless you can help us with financing.

No animals were harmed or consumed in the writing of this Rembis Report.

XV

Summer

Sent: Saturday, June 02, 2007 2:38 AM
Subject: The Rembis Report - Volume XV

Today, I decided that I had procrastinated long enough about obtaining a Montana drivers license. I have lived here over a year and with this most recent address change and the prodding of my dear sweet wife to "do the right thing" I paid a visit to the halls of justice or whatever they call that municipal building, pulled a paper number from the counter, and waited an excruciating 40 minutes for my turn. It was a normal transaction. The clerk took my payment and returned my Florida license with a hole punched through it as a souvenir of the day I changed residency. Everything was going fine. Then she told me to smile. I stood before the camera, culminating everything I had learned professionally about posing for my picture and gave her 32 pearly whites, dimples and cheekbones and she said to me "We don't do that here."

"What?" I queried.

"You need to make a normal face."

Now, I wasn't just stunned. I was hurt. "This is my normal face. This is what I look like." I told her, and she snapped the picture while I was talking. Sadly, my new drivers license photo is a travesty. It is a bastardization of the real me. The only consolation I have is that it will be safely tucked away in my wallet and displayed only when I need to rent a car or some other rare occasion to a clerk who will not care and most likely won't notice the picture.

But I should have been ready for this. Many Montanans are intimidated by people with teeth and symmetrical facial features. It makes for a moment I will not soon forget.

There is something else I cannot forget. I know exactly where I was and what I was doing 20 years ago today. Today, June 1st, is a special occasion. Not just to me, but to many people for many personal reasons. Here's a few:

On June 1st in

1812 U.S. President James Madison warned Congress that war with Britain was imminent. The War of 1812 started 17 days later.

1880 The first public pay telephone began operation in New Haven, Connecticut.

1964 The U.S. Supreme Court banned prayers and Bible teaching in public schools on the constitutional grounds of separation of church and state.

1968 Helen Keller, who became a world-renowned author and lecturer despite being blind and deaf from infancy, died in Westport, Connecticut, at the age of 87.

1973 Greek Prime Minister George Papadopoulos abolished the Greek monarchy and proclaimed Greece a republic with himself as president.

1990 U.S. President George H.W. Bush and Soviet leader Mikhail Gorbachev agreed to sharp cuts in chemical and nuclear weapons.

The South African government proposed a bill to scrap the 37-year-old law segregating buses, trains, toilets, libraries, swimming pools and other public amenities.

1991 Secretary of State James Baker and Soviet Foreign Minister Aleksandr Bessmertnykh resolved their differences over a conventional weapons reduction treaty.

1993 The Guatemalan military, acting in response to appeals from the judiciary and the public, ousted President Jorge Serrano Elias from office. President Dobrica Cosic of Yugoslavia was voted out of office by the Parliament.

1997 French parliamentary elections brought parties of the left into power for the first time since 1986.

2003 With hostilities continuing in Iraq, coalition leaders decided against creating a large national assembly soon but rather devised a plan for an advisory council of 25 to 30 Iraqis instead.

2004 Oil prices jumped to $42.33 a barrel, highest reported at that time, before falling back.

2005 Dutch voters joined France in overwhelmingly rejecting the proposed European Union constitution.

I know what you're thinking; so what?

Just because it's trivia doesn't make it interesting, and you're right. If it's not your birthday or some other significant anniversary I am certain you're not jumping up and down because this is the day that prayer was banned in public school or the Greek monarchy was abolished. Okay, maybe not all of you, but most of you aren't celebrating for any particular reason today. I myself am not celebrating any more than by writing this memoir, but I am proud to say that I do remember where I was 20 years ago today in 1987.

I was driving across the country in my 1976 Olds Cutlass. It was a puke green beast with a white vinyl top and a 442 under the hood. The rust on the quarter panels was like Swiss cheese; you could see right through the trunk to the other side. The week before I took it to visit my old neighborhood and its birthplace, Detroit.

That's my childhood best friend Vytas Norkunas behind the wheel and it was the last time I saw him. On June 1st, I started the day near the South Dakota/Wyoming border somewhere off I-90. I had slept in the car that night under the pitch of a moonless night and infinite specs of starlight.

I was on my way to Yellowstone Park, simply to find a new life, and perhaps myself I guess, even though I wasn't looking. I had driven all the way from Florida solo save for a kitten I named Traveler. We spent the day before exploring the Badlands and Mount Rushmore.

Then we drove over the Bighorn Mountains along US 14 to Greybull. I took an icy bath on the side of the road in Shell Creek and Traveler stayed beside me, obedient as a dog, waiting on the bank. On the way to Cody, I saw a coyote for the very first time. It jaunted across the road and into a field, careless of our presence.

Later in the day, I came to the east entrance of Yellowstone Park. I didn't know there would be a ranger at the gate. It felt a bit like crossing into another country, but I didn't need to show any ID. I was worried they wouldn't let me bring Traveler in, so I hid him under a jacket. I paid my fee, got a park map and we rolled right in. We were in the clear, baby, right past the fuzz. We stopped at several pullouts and saw mud pots, bison, elk, the Grand Canyon of the Yellowstone, and Lake Yellowstone. It was great.

Traveler especially liked Tower Falls.

When it got dark we parked just west of Tower intending to bed down for the night. But something near tragic happened. Traveler chose to utilize his litter box and did so with such gusto that the Olds Cutlass was now fouled terribly. Of course I emptied the box, but the smell did not go away. The only way to air it out was to drive with the windows down part way and rush a breeze through there.

Exhibit J
Vytautas Norkunas driving my Oldsmobile Cutlass Supreme in Detroit, Michigan, 1987

Exhibit K
Traveler at Badlands National Park, South Dakota

Exhibit L
Traveler at Mount Rushmore National Memorial, South Dakota

Exhibit M
Traveler at Cody, Wyoming

Exhibit N
Traveler at Tower Falls, Yellowstone National Park, Wyoming

In about twenty minutes, we came to Mammoth Hot Springs. I stopped to visit the bar and left Traveler in the car to enjoy himself in all his odorous glory.

The bartender suggested I go down to Gardiner Montana, just five miles away, if I really wanted to find a pool table. So I did. When I got there I met some good people who invited me up to their trailer so I wouldn't have to stay in my car that night. I accepted that offer and wound up deciding to spend the summer in Gardiner.

I met my wife-to-be, Ellen, a few weeks later and spent the next two years living there.

I didn't keep a diary to know where I was that day. It was the radio. As I drove from Greybull to Cody, the radio station was celebrating the 20th anniversary of the Beatles album Sgt. Pepper's Lonely Hearts Club Band. They played the whole album and featured interviews with the Beatles and other notable celebrities. That drive etched itself into my mind to such an extent that I could never forget where I was on the first day of June in 1987.

Now, 20 years later, Sgt. Pepper is 40 and my cat, my car, and my friend Vytas are cherished still frame memories of youth kept alive by the turn of a calendar. Oddly enough, I am yet again only a few miles away from Yellowstone Park. Although a visit to the drivers license office is certainly not high adventure nor the warmest of reminiscences, it does give me another story to tell about what happened to me one June 1st.

I'd like to invite you all to see that toothy grin that scares the natives out here at my website. You can read about and watch a few minutes of BEST and see what else I am capable of when you give me internet software. You'd better check it out. I gave some of you folks links to your own websites and associations like this may ruin your reputations. I really don't want that to happen, so if there's some link that you don't think deserves to be on my site, please let me know so I can tell people not to click that one.

Other newsmakers this month include one of my BESTest friends Georgia Chris who has a movie trailer out and Maureen Smithorbob had another article published at the online women's mag Who Is Isabella?

As for me, I am keeping my fingers crossed for some screenplay competitions I am currently entered in and will keep you posted on any success. I'd say more but I don't want to jinx it.

Keep me posted too, on your endeavors and triumphs, so I can tell the whole world about them here at The Rembis Report.

Ciao

Mike Rembis

HAPPY JUNE 1ST!

Yeah, I know. It's June 2nd now. Give me a break.

From The Response File
Volume XV

Received: Monday, June 4, 2007 10:54 PM
Mike,

Once again I'm going to clue you in on something incredibly trivial. Here it is. July 2nd of every year is the day in the middle of the year. (except leap years) That means 182 days have passed and there are 182 more to come. Why they don't have a holiday out of it I'll never know.

D.D.

My Reply:
Dan,

That IS incredibly trivial, I'm glad you told me so that I can look like a geek this July 2nd when I tell everyone I meet.

Wait a minute. Did I just accidentally infer that you're a geek? If I did. I'm sorry. I really don't think of you as a geek, just trivial. No, not trivial as in not important, but somebody who seems to know a lot of unimportant things. Not that what you have to say isn't important, it's not. I mean, it is, important, but not because you said it, it's important because it's a fact.

I hope I have made myself perfectly clear and you don't think of me as a geek.

Because I'm not.
I think.
Mike

Dan's Reply:
Mike,
Well....if you like trivial stuff you'll really dig this. Before I read that last message of yours, I received another one from a guy who talked about how one of the secrets of happiness is how not to take anything so personally. I deleted it but now I wish I didn't. Besides, if anything is geekish about me it's the fact that I like Star Wars, Lord of the Rings, I wear glasses, and I don't date much even though women in general find me likable. Everything else is cool. Hahaha!
D.D.

My Reply:
Speaking of secrets, a few of my friends have recently told me I needed to read The Secret and see the movie. I thought to myself, if it's a secret, why are they broadcasting it? Then I read this article on Salon.com:

Oprah's Ugly Secret
By continuing to hawk "The Secret," a mishmash of offensive self-help cliches, Oprah Winfrey is squandering her goodwill and influence, and preaching to the world that mammon is queen.
by Peter Birkenhead

Steve Martin used to do a routine that went like this: "You too can be a millionaire! It's easy: First, get a million dollars. Now..."

If you put that routine between hard covers, you'd have "The Secret," the self-help manifesto and bottle of minty-fresh snake oil currently topping the bestseller lists. "The Secret" espouses a "philosophy" patched together by an Australian talk-show producer named Rhonda Byrne. Though "The Secret" unabashedly appropriates and mishmashes familiar self-help clichés, it was still the subject of two recent episodes of "The Oprah Winfrey Show" featuring a dream team of self-help gurus, all of whom contributed to the project.

The main idea of "The Secret" is that people need only visualize what they want in order to get it — and the book certainly has created instant wealth, at least for Rhonda Byrne and her partners-in-con. And the marketing idea behind it — the enlisting of that dream team, in what is essentially a massive, cross-promotional pyramid scheme — is brilliant.

But what really makes "The Secret" more than a variation on an old theme is the involvement of Oprah Winfrey, who lends the whole enterprise more prestige, and, because of that prestige, more venality, than any previous self-help scam. Oprah hasn't just endorsed "The Secret"; she's championed it, put herself at the apex of its pyramid, and helped create a symbiotic economy of New Age quacks that almost puts OPEC to shame.

Why "venality"? Because, with survivors of Auschwitz still alive, Oprah writes this about "The Secret" on her Web site, "the energy you put into the world — both good and bad — is exactly what comes back to you. This means you create the circumstances of your life with the choices you make every day." "Venality," because Oprah, in the age of AIDS, is advertising a book that says, "You cannot 'catch' anything unless you think you can and thinking you can is inviting it to you with your thought." "Venality," because Oprah, from a studio within walking distance of Chicago's notorious Cabrini Green Projects, pitches a book that says, "The only reason any person does not have enough money is because they are blocking money from coming to them with their thoughts."

Worse than "The Secret's" blame-the-victim idiocy is its bald-faced bullshitting. The titular "secret" of the book is something the authors call the Law of Attraction. They maintain that the universe is governed by the principle that "like attracts like" and that our thoughts are like magnets: Positive thoughts attract positive events and negative thoughts attract negative events. Of course, magnets do exactly the opposite — positively charged magnets attract negatively charged particles — and the rest of "The Secret" has a similar relationship to the truth. Here it is on biblical history: "Abraham, Isaac, Jacob, Joseph, Moses, and Jesus were not only prosperity teachers, but also millionaires themselves, with more affluent lifestyles than many present-day millionaires could conceive of." And worse than the idiocy and the bullshitting is its anti-intellectualism because that's at the root of the other two. Here's "The Secret" on reading and, um, electricity: "When I discovered 'The Secret' I made a decision that I would not watch the news or read newspapers anymore, because it did not make me feel good," and, "How does it work? Nobody knows. Just like nobody knows how electricity works. I don't, do you?" And worst of all is the craven consumerist worldview at the heart of "The Secret," because it's why the book exists: "[The Secret] is like having the Universe as your catalogue. You flip through it and say, 'I'd like to have this experience and I'd like to have that product and I'd like to have a person like that.' It is you placing your order with the Universe. It's really that easy." That's from Dr. Joe Vitale, former Amway executive and contributor to "The Secret," on Oprah.com.

Oprah Winfrey is one of the richest women in the world, and one of the most influential. Her imprimatur has helped the authors of "The Secret" sell 2 million books (and 1 million DVDs), putting it ahead of the new Harry Potter book on the Amazon bestseller list. In the time Oprah spent advertising the lies in "The Secret," she could have been exposing them to an audience that otherwise might have believed them. So why didn't she? If James Frey deserved to be raked over the coals for lying about how drunk he was, doesn't Oprah deserve some scrutiny for pitching the meretricious nonsense in "The Secret"?

Oprah has a reputation for doing good — she probably has more perceived moral authority than anyone in this country — and she has done a lot of good. But in light of her zealous support of a book that says, in this time of entrenched, systemic, institutionalized poverty, this time of no-bid contracts for war profiteers and heckuva-job governance, that "you can have, be, or do anything," isn't it reasonable to ask about why she does what she does, and the way she does it?

Oprah recently opened, with much fanfare, the Oprah Winfrey Leadership Academy in South Africa, and as I watched the network news stories about it, I couldn't get "The Secret" out of my mind. I kept wondering what would happen if Professor Sam Mhlongo, South Africa's chief family practitioner who famously said that HIV doesn't cause AIDS, read about Oprah's connection to "The Secret" and found support there for his claim. I wondered if the students of the academy would read "The Secret" and start to believe that their parents deserved to be poor, or that the people of Darfur summoned the Janjaweed with "bad thoughts." Will the heavier girls be told, as readers of "The Secret" are, that food doesn't cause weight gain — thinking about weight gain does? Will they be told to not even look at fat people, as "The Secret" advises? Oprah is already promoting these ideas to her television audience. Why wouldn't she espouse them to her students?

In many ways the Leadership Academy is a wonderful project, a school that will provide impoverished girls an education they otherwise might not have gotten. But it also seems to be the product, unavoidably, of the faux-spiritual, anti-intellectual, hyper-materialistic worldview expressed in "The Secret," the book that the school's founder has called "life changing."

The academy is a controversial enough project in South Africa that the government withdrew its support, because of the amount of money that's been spent on its well-reported, lavish design — money that could have gone instead to creating perfectly fine schools that served many, many more students than the 350 who will be making use of spa facilities at the academy. But, when I watched Oprah's prime-time special about interviewing candidates for the school, it seemed to me that she wasn't nearly as excited about providing an education to the girls as she was about providing a "Secret"-like "transformative experience." (And not just for the girls, for herself; the first thing she said to the family members at the opening ceremony wasn't, "Welcome to a great moment in your daughters' lives," it was, "Welcome to the proudest moment of my life.")

On the special, Oprah talked far more about what the school would do for the girls' self-esteem and material lives than what it would do for their intellects — sometimes sounding as if she was reading directly from "The Secret." And in discussing what she was looking for in prospective students, she didn't talk about finding the next Eleanor Roosevelt or Sally Ride or Jane Smiley. Instead she used "Entertainment Tonight" language like "It Girl" to describe her ideal candidate. She praised the girls for their spirit, for how much they "shined" and "glowed," but never for their ideas or insights. Oprah puts a lot of energy and money into aesthetics — on her show, in her magazine, at her school. The publishers of "The Secret" have learned well from their sponsor and are just as visually savvy. They have created a look for their books, DVDs, CDs, and marketing materials that conjures a "Da Vinci Code" aesthetic, full of pretty faux parchment, quill-and-ink fonts, and wax seals.

Oprah's TV special about the Leadership Academy, essentially an hourlong infomercial, was just as well-coiffed and "visuals"-heavy. In fact, when Oprah was choosing her students, her important criteria must have included their television interview skills. On-camera interviews with the girls were the centerpiece of the special, but as one spunky, telegenic candidate after another beamed her smile at the camera, I couldn't help wondering how Joyce Carol Oates or Gertrude Stein or Madame Curie would have fared — would they have "shined" and "glowed," or more likely talked in non-sound-bite-friendly paragraphs and maybe even, God forbid, the sometimes "dark" tones of authentic people, and been rejected. Sadly, the girls themselves (and who can blame them, desperate 12-year-olds trying to flatter their potential benefactor) parroted banal Oprah-isms, like "I want to be the best me I can be," and "Be a leader not a follower" and "Don't blend in, blend out," with smiley gusto.

When the special was over, I found myself equally impressed and queasy, one part hopeful, one part worried. I was happy the school was there but disturbed by the way it created an instant upper class out of the students, in a country that doesn't exactly need any more segregation into haves and have-nots. I was hopeful for the students but nervous about what, exactly, they will be taught in a place called the Oprah Winfrey Leadership Academy. Will it be more "best me I can be" bromides? Will "The Secret" be on the syllabus? Oprah herself is going to teach "leadership classes" at the school, after all.

Has Oprah ever done anything that didn't leave people with mixed feelings?

And at what point do we stop feeling like we have to take the good with the craven when it comes to Oprah, and the culture she's helped to create? I get nauseated when I think of people in South Africa being taught they don't have enough money because they're "blocking it with their thoughts." I'm already sickened by an American culture that teaches people, as "The Secret" does, that they "create the circumstances of their lives with the choices they make every day," a culture that elected a president who cried tears of self-congratulation at his inauguration, rejects intellectualism, and believes he can intuit the trustworthiness of world leaders by looking into their eyes. I'm sickened by a culture in which the tenets of the Oprah philosophy have become conventional wisdom, in which genuine self-actualization has been confused with self-aggrandizement, reality is whatever you want it to be, and mammon is queen.

One of Oprah's signature gimmicks has been giving stuff away to her audience ("giving" here means announcing the passing of stuff from corporate sponsors to audience members), most notably in a popular segment called "My Favorite Things." These bits have revealed an Oprah who truly revels in consumer culture, and who can seem astonishingly oblivious to the way most people live and what they can afford. She seems to celebrate every event and milestone with extravagant stuff, indeed, to not know how to celebrate without it. Oprah has explained the expensive appointments of her Leadership Academy by saying, "Beauty inspires." True enough. But hasn't the lack of beauty inspired some pretty great work? And aren't there are all kinds of beauty?

You might expect a powerful person who thinks of herself as "deeply spiritual" to have a less worldly conception of it, and you might hope that she would encourage her followers to do the same, instead of urging them to buy books that call Jesus a "prosperity teacher."

But, far more than "spiritual growth" or "empowerment," Oprah and the authors of "The Secret" focus on imparting the message of getting rich. Even the biographies of the authors of "The Secret" on Oprah's Web site are revealingly fixated on their rags-to-riches stories. James Arthur Ray is described as someone who was "almost going bankrupt, [which] forced him to focus on the life he truly wanted. Now he runs a multi-million-dollar corporation dedicated to teaching people how to create wealth in all areas of their lives." The bio for Lisa Nichols says, "After hitting rock bottom at age

19, Lisa prayed for a better life. Now, she has made her fortune by motivating more than 60,000 teenagers to make better choices in their own lives." And the one for "Chicken Soup for the Soul" creator Jack Canfield reads, he "was deep in debt before he made it big. Now his best-selling books have sold more than 100 million copies worldwide, and Jack travels the country teaching 'The Secret' of his success."

There's no doubt that Oprah's doing a lot of good with her South African project, and with many other charitable works. And yeah, I know, her book club "gets people to read," and yadda yadda yadda. But there's also no doubt that a lot of us have been making forgiving disclaimers like that about Oprah for years. And that maybe they amount to trains-running-on-time arguments. Maybe it's time to stop. After reading "The Secret," it seemed to me that there were basically three possibilities: 1) Oprah really believes this stuff, and we should be very worried about her opening a school for anyone. 2) Oprah doesn't believe this stuff and we should be very, very worried about her opening a school for anyone. 3) Oprah doesn't know that any of this stuff is in the book or on her Web site and in a perfect world she wouldn't be allowed to open a school for anyone.

The things that Oprah does, like promoting "The Secret," can seem deceptively trivial, but it's precisely because they're silly that we should be concerned about their promotion by someone who is deadly earnest and deeply trusted by millions of people. It's important to start taking a look at Oprah because her philosophy has in many ways become the dominant one in our culture, even for people who would never consider themselves disciples. Somebody is buying enough copies of "The Secret" to make it No. 1 on the Amazon bestseller list. Those somebodies may be religious zealots or atheists, Republicans or Democrats, but they are all believers, to one degree or another, and, perhaps unwittingly, in aspects of the Oprah/"Secret" culture. And yes, sure, a lot of the believing they do is harmless fun — everybody's got some kind of rabbit's foot in his pocket — but we're not talking about rabbits' feet here, we're talking about whole, live rabbits pulled out of hats, and an audience that doesn't think it's being tricked.

"Secret"-style belief is a perfect product. Like Coca-Cola, it goes down easy and makes the consumer thirsty for more. It's unthreateningly simple, and a lot more facile, sentimental and, perhaps paradoxically, intractable than the old-fashioned kind of belief. Like Amway, it enlists its consumers as unofficial salespeople, and the people who constitute its market feel like they're part of a fold. It's indistinguishable from, and inextricably bound up in, the Oprah idea of self-esteem, the kind of confidence you get not from testing yourself, but from "believing" in yourself. This modern idea of faith isn't arrived at the old-fashioned way, by asking questions, but by getting answers. Instead of inquiry we have born-again epiphanies and cheesy self-help books — we have excuses for not engaging in inquiry at all. Let other people schlep down the road to Damascus; we'll have Amazon send Damascus to us.

That "Secret"-style faith, whether it's in God, or in one's own preordained destiny to be an "American Idol," which takes all of a moment to achieve, is perhaps its most important selling point. Here's "The Secret" on arriving at faith: "Ask once, believe you have received, and all you have to do to receive is feel good." The kind of faith that couldn't be reached by shortcut, the confidence of the great doubters and worriers, of Moses and Abraham Lincoln and Jesus Christ, has been replaced by the insta-certainty and inflated "self-esteem" of "The Secret's" believers.

Books like "The Secret" have created, and are feeding, an enormously diverse market of disciples, and they're thriving in every corner of the culture, in megachurches and movies, politics and pop music, in sports arenas and state boards of education. Oprah has far more in common with George Bush than either would like to admit, and so do the psychics of Marin County, California, and the creationists of Kansas. The believers come from all walks of life, but they work the same way — mostly by bastardizing and warping source materials, from the Bible to the Bhagavad Gita, to make them fit their worldview. On Page 23 of "The Secret" you'll find this revealing doozy: "Meditation quiets the mind, helps you control your thoughts." Of course, the goal of meditation is precisely the opposite — it is to be conscious, to observe your thoughts honestly and clearly. But that's the last thing the believers want to encourage. The authors of "The Secret" sell "control" in the form of "empowerment" and "quiet" in the form of belief, not consciousness.

The promises of Oprah culture can seem irresistible, and its hallmarks are becoming ubiquitous. Believers may be separated into tribes according to what they believe, but they do it in pretty much the same way, relying on a "Secret"-style conception of "intuition" — which seems to amount to the sneaking suspicion that they're always right — to arrive at their tenets. Instead of the world as it is, constantly changing and full of contradiction, they see a fixed and fantastical place, where good things come to those who believe, whether it's belief in a diet, a God, or a Habit of Successful People. These believers may believe in the healing power of homeopathy, or Scripture or organizational skills — in intelligent design, astrology, or privatization. They all trust that their devotion will be rewarded with money and boyfriends and job promotions, with hockey championships and apartments. And most of all they believe — they really, really believe — in themselves.

For these believers, self-knowledge is much less important than self-"love." But the question they never seem to ask themselves is: If you wouldn't tell another person, you loved her before you got to know her, why would you do that to yourself? Skipping the getting-to-know-you part has given us what we deserve: the Oprah culture.

It's a culture where superstition is "spirituality," illiteracy is "authenticity," and schoolmarm moralism is "character." It's a culture where people apologize by saying, "I'm sorry you took offense at what I said," and forgive by saying, "I'm not angry at you anymore, I'm grateful to you for teaching me not to trust shitheads like you." And that's the part that should bother us most: the diminishing, even implicit mocking, of genuine goodness, and of authentic spiritual concerns and practices. Engagement, curiosity, and active awe are in short supply these days, and it's sickening to see them devalued and misrepresented.

Not that any of this is new. Aimee Semple McPherson, "The Power of Positive Thinking," Father Coughlin, Est (Erhard Seminars Training), James Van Praagh — pick your influential snake-oil salesman or snake oil. They were all cut from the same cloth as Oprah and "The Secret." The big, big difference is, well, the bigness. The infinitely bigger reach of the Oprah empire and its emissaries. They make their predecessors look like kids with lemonade stands. It would be stupidly dangerous to dismiss Oprah and "The Secret" as silly, or ultimately meaningless. They're reaching more people than Harry Potter, for God-force's sake. That's why what Oprah does matters, and stinks. If you reach more people than Bill O'Reilly, if you have better name recognition than Nelson Mandela, if the books you endorse sell more than Stephen King's, you should take some responsibility for your effect on the culture. The most powerful woman in the world is taking advantage of people who are desperate for meaning, by passionately championing a product that mocks the very idea of a meaningful life.

That means something.

Peter Birkenhead is a writer living in Los Angeles[5]

More from Me:
> Do you think we'd make any money if we started telling people about the secrets of how to become an extremely wealthy successful geek, or did Bill Gates beat us to it?
>
> Considering the fact that we're not really geeks, I guess that doesn't make us authorities anyway, but it was a train of thought.
>
> I'm trying not to think about the extremely wealthy part.
>
> Mike

Dan's Reply:
> That's a good question. If we had the secrets of wealth, we could theoretically become wealthy. But only if we use them right. I believe it's one thing to have the right knowledge and another thing to put in the effort to do it. Hence the old saying *"Genius is 1 percent inspiration and 99 percent perspiration."*[6] For example, I can play basketball but that doesn't make me Michael Jordan.
>
> You're right about the secret part. I feel the same way about the secret service. If the government has an organization that does the same stuff as the secret service but hasn't mentioned it to the rest of the world, they are the REAL secret service. I'll bet they're a bunch of geeks. D.D

XVI

Seeds in the Wind

Sent: Sunday, July 01, 2007 11:52 AM
Subject: The Rembis Report - Volume XVI

The latest bane of my existence are the alleged automatic sprinklers that water our lawn. Like most irrigation systems, they work on a timer, and are set to water at specific times for set periods. I can't explain why, but our sprinklers do not comprehend this concept. Sometimes they work fine and sometimes they gurgle into sad fountainous geysers that don't spray in the semi-circles they are programmed for, instead, flooding the sidewalk or a portion of the lawn and creating a haven for mosquito larvae. I am watching them now. A moment ago, Valve # 1 was having a difficult morning, as though it needed coffee and a brisk walk, and now Valve # 2 is performing properly, just having a party with the birds. How will Valve # 's 3-6 behave? We'll see. Of course, I tried to have a professional certified Rain-Bird guy come out to check the system, but like all other people you call for help when you reach for the Yellow Pages, he never called back. Of course, if he were reliable enough to not need to advertise to find new business, he would most likely be too busy to deal with a new customer and I would be right where I am anyway, staring out the window watching my lawn like a gambler at the races praying for a clean run and a strong finish.

You get all kinds of surprises when you test the old equipment in your new home. Not just the plumbing, but light switches that don't turn anything on, bedroom doors that lock you in, plugged gutters with their own ecosystems and weather patterns. In my exploration below the floorboards in the crawlspace of our house, I discovered not only decades of trash discarded by workmen, old spools of wire, scraps of sheet metal and unused ductwork, but in fact, the entire original furnace, lying there, defunct. Since there is really no need to go down there other than changing an air filter or to work on wiring or cable lines, it's not in the way and I have no real need to retrieve it and haul it off, so there it will stay, a time capsule of trash, protected from the elements and preserved for posterity as a testament to laziness, not only to myself, but to the guys who left it there.

Crawling about, my flashlight spied a cardboard box. Since it was not too far out of the way I decided to investigate. Lo and behold, I opened the box to discover about a hundred identical cassette tapes, all neatly packaged in plastic and ready for sale. SCORE! Finders Keepers, that's the way I was raised. It's my house, I own 'em! It is evident from the name on the tapes that this album was self produced by the man who grew up in this house, Dave Whearty.

In 1991, Dave Whearty produced his album Seeds In The Wind. He describes it as a one hour sing-along of 21st century folk music. I have not yet listened to it, but am intrigued by the playlist:

Let's Sing Together
I'm Somebody Fine

Just Tryin' To Be Myself
I'm OK, You're OK

Exhibit O
Seeds in the Wind by Dave Whearty

We're Friends Friends Friends
We're The Foundation
The Justice Of The People
We Shall Be Free
'Til Tyranny And Misery Are Gone
Raise The Flag Of Justice
Step By Step
Ba Da Da
Let The Precious Children Shine
Let's Plant This Tree
I Will Care For The Land
Oo Ba Da
Song Of Youth
Going Our Way
Have You Heard The Sunrise ?

From inside the cover:
ABOUT THE SONGWRITER
Dave Whearty was born in 1949 and lives in his hometown of Billings, Montana. He is an Eagle Scout, a Vietnam War Conscientious Objector, and is a graduate of Rocky Mountain College and Kansas State University. He has been a journeyman baker, an SGI member, and a songwriter for many years.
Copyright 1991 Dave Whearty

There is also an address to send $11 plus $1 shipping and handling to get another cassette with two songbooks, but my friends, readers of the Rembis Report, have I got a deal for you! I'll send you a cassette and 2 songbooks for the low, low price of $10 plus $1 shipping and handling. I believe these are very rare editions that you cannot buy in stores. I didn't see it listed on BMG. There is one review I found for what was apparently a second album by Dave Whearty,

Secret Of The Soil and apparently, Dave Whearty is involved with the website Circle of Joy. So for those of you with cassette players, I'd say that this album is a must have! And, if you don't have a cassette player, my friends, you're in luck, they still sell them on the internet. There is no good reason you can't start enjoying this 20th Century Folk Music in about a week or two. (That's how long shipping would take after we cash your check.) This exclusive offer is being made only through The Rembis Report, and I don't have enough for all of you, so it's first come, first served. That's the only way to be fair.

If 20th Century Folk Music is not your thing, you might like to check out what one of my BESTest friends Jill has been up to at her new website. On the writing front, I was extremely fortunate to be one of ten finalists in the Boston International Film Festival Screenplay to Production contest. I was informed of this through a personal email and it was not published anywhere, the way they published the finalists list on their website last year when in that same competition I was a runner up with Blondzilla. I entered the third draft in that competition and will be editing it into a fourth draft based on the reviews I have received on TriggerStreet as they relate to the second draft. I have a lot of ideas to implement and make it a smoother read.

Don't think for a second that my efforts are going to wind up forgotten in a basement. I'm going to keep sputtering along until I get it right and get my stories out there.

That reminds me, I need to work on my sprinklers.

XVII

Fort Benton

Sent: Tuesday, July 31, 2007 9:49 PM
Subject: The Rembis Report - Volume XVII

Main Street, Fort Benton, Montana was once renowned as the bloodiest street in the West, a haven of lawlessness where gunfights became the norm. The main industries were gambling and prostitution to appease newcomers to the West. This is where I am today. As you may have surmised by now, as of this writing, I am still alive. I survived the night in the hotel.

I wasn't sure that I would however, when I checked into the Pioneer Lodge. It was clean and reasonably priced, and traveling any further last night would have made no sense for my routine, so I stopped. I was escorted by the ancient matronly desk clerk to room #4, right down the hall. A quiet interior room with a window to the hallway, but none to the outside, so that if in the wee hours of the morning, close to sunrise, if I were cornered by a vampire, I would be utterly defenseless when ripping down the curtain to reveal an interior filled with artificial light instead of the pure cosmic rays of the sun. I suppose it was this absolute terror that made me ask "Do you have a room with a window?"

She told me, "Well, we do have one room, but it's upstairs and we don't have an elevator to it."

"That's okay. As long as it has a window."

"It does, but it's on the second floor, and it looks out over the alley." she tried again to deter me to no avail.

"Great."

"Most people don't like this room."

"Why? Is it haunted?"

"It's a very special room."

"Okay. So does that mean it's haunted?"

"Do you want a haunted room?"

"I don't know - no not particularly."

"This room has a lot of memories."

I was fearful of asking if a family was slaughtered in that particular room and never realized until later that she had deftly avoided answering the question of haunting. The key had no number on it, nor did the door at the top of the stairs in the back. "What number is this room."

"We just call it the bedroom. If you're claustrophobic, this is where you go."

So there I was. In the bedroom. An L-shaped room with a massive bookshelf overlooking two beds. One on each end of the L. Next to one bed, across from the many books, paperbacks mostly, was a mirrored closet door with the bed so close, the closet was unusable. Behind the other bed was the bathroom with a walk-in glass shower, toilet and mirrors. The bathroom had windows, as did both beds. The books and knick-knacks were extremely personal items, so it was like being in someone's home rather than a hotel.

I chose the bed closer to the bathroom than the books and mirror. Above it on the windowsill stands a white porcelain goddess holding a bounty of grapes. Her expression is of an innocent child and she stares at the bed. Atop the glass case next to her is a figurine of a Native American warrior, like a doll. Inside the case, smaller figurines of cartoon like children and geodes and an alabaster case, a motley showcase of things acquired over a lifetime and placed in random order because one has run out of space elsewhere.

There was a sewing table with a machine sunk down inside. The drawers were filled with thread and swatches and giant sharp scissors and needles and other implements of destruction. If I could get to the scissors before the ax murderer got in the door I would be safe. Then there were the books.

About a thousand books adorned the shelves that ran the entire length of the room. A library without the benefit of the Dewey decimal system, although it was neat, the books were in no particular order. Sometimes volumes that belonged together were, like the Reader's Digest condensed editions or those of a particular author. Inside the doors of the case were old phonograph records mostly by artists I had never heard of with posed photographs on their covers that screamed of Americana. Most were in pristine condition, like the books.

Most of the books looked like they had never or only been read once with their owner's name inscribed on the inside covers. When you are stuck in a room full of books, it is inevitable that you search the titles for what you have read and take note of almost everything. Like any hotel room, curiosity draws you to every crevice and drawer and I soon discovered that I was looking through somebody's past. There were high school yearbooks from both 1955 and 1972. The books were both popular and unknown. I searched for my favorite authors, Peter Benchley and Joseph Heller and found neither, but I did notice The Adventures of Tom Sawyer by Mark Twain, Ulysses by James Joyce, and the Bible, to name a few you may have heard of. Atlas Shrugged by Ayn Rand, and several novels by Robin Cook and Dean Koontz, but nothing by Stephen King. Then I saw In Cold Blood by Truman Capote.

When I used to read a great deal more than I do now, I would go to the library and look for the last book I read and find the book on the shelf directly to its right. Most times, I would pick up this book and read it, because my theory was that if I did this consistently enough, I would eventually read everything that existed. Some volumes I would completely gloss over and go to the next one or find another way to choose what to read. This system did have its benefits, mainly being that it got me to read all of Joseph Heller's novels and many editions by Tom Robbins, Mark Twain, Robert Louis Stevenson, and Kurt Vonnegut, Jr. These became major influences for my personal love of sarcasm and my writing. I never did read everything, but I read a lot. There were books I had forced on me by school that I had to read and one in particular that my father wanted me to read that I wouldn't - a bizarre book that Pat Boone wrote in 1958 about teenage angst. In 1978 I had absolutely no interest in what Pat Boone had to say twenty years prior.

The last book I read was Hotel by Arthur Hailey. No, not the guy who wrote Roots, that was Alex Haley. Arthur Hailey wrote an exhaustive 400+ page treatise on the inner workings of the fictional St. Gregory Hotel in 1962 New Orleans. Not only did he focus on fantastic character development, but he brought forth themes such as corruption and civil rights to show how society really worked in that day and age.

One book that was cutting edge for its time was Truman Capote's In Cold Blood, still hailed as a masterpiece, it dramatizes the horrific murder of a simple family in Kansas by two young rogues. The scariest thing about it is the idea that it could happen to anyone and more frightening still, knowing that it does. Fictional killers like Norman Bates of Psycho are disturbingly real entities in our world.

The next book that I have on my bookshelf at home happens to be In Cold Blood. I haven't started reading it yet, but that is my intention now that I have finished Hotel. Since it was right there in my room I reached for it. When I took it off the shelf, right there next to it was Hotel. In perfect sequence Hotel, then In Cold Blood, just like my bookshelf at home. Suddenly, this felt like more than a coincidence. I looked at the rest of this particular shelf and discovered that many of these bindings held books that I had already read or had some odd connection with. Down on the end, Jacqueline Suzanne's Valley of the Dolls, which had shocked somebody, I forget who, that I was reading it as an adolescent. Nestled above that was J.D. Salinger's Catcher in the Rye, also something I read as a youth. I always seemed to steer toward reading things other kids my age would never touch simply because there was no way for them to relate to it. Right next to Valley of the Dolls sat Irwin Shaw's Rich Man, Poor Man, another of those unrelatable epics I had absorbed. Quite simply, this bookshelf creeped me out because it made me feel as if I belonged here and to me, that is not a good feeling to have when it's a place I never particularly planned to go. The next thing I noticed was the novel that had been rewritten for the stage and was one of the high school plays I performed in - Up The Down Staircase. Then, like an unexpected curve in the road at 90 MPH, Pat Boone's advice novelette: Twixt 12 and 20. I felt a bit sick, because right down from that was another book my Dad wanted me to read that I wouldn't, Dale Carnegie's How to Win Friends and Influence People. There were two copies of this one.

Had I been destined to be in this room for some bizarre reason? Does this mean something? I wondered.

I was born on September 2, 1964 at 1:05 AM.

I reeled back to take stock of my life and whether or not

pre-destiny existed. I thought hard about it. Why would these books be arranged on this bookshelf in this order? I had read about half the shelf. Does that mean when I finish the shelf, I'll be done? Or ready for another shelf?

I took pictures with my digital camera of everything in the room so I could study it later. Because I am on the road I am unable to upload anything to you now, but have included a few photos for your delight to show you how public bathrooms are decorated in Montana, some lovely countryside near Glacier National Park and Don Quixote's nightmare, the field of windmills near Judith Gap.

Fearful of the room full of books and not knowing why, I went for a walk across the street along the banks of the Missouri River and read all of the historical markers. That's how I learned it was once the bloodiest street in the west and that the building I was to sleep in with the words of thousands of authors surrounding me was one of the oldest buildings in Fort Benton and served as the first department store after being built in 1882. But what happened in that department store, exactly? I was certain the only person who could possibly answer that question would be Stephen King. Since there were no King books on the shelves, he had to be the one in charge of this little chapter of my life because, although he may write about authors, he never writes himself into his own stories.

Then the warm breeze became a hot wind. Forest fires burning miles away from here were most certainly being fueled further and I felt something sting my cheek. It wasn't rain. It was ash. Some rain followed a moment later. The wind gusted around 50 MPH, bending trees, and squalling the river water. It only lasted a few minutes. I went to dinner at a place called Bob's, where they unfortunately chill the red wine, but the meal was okay. It was dark when I came back out and the wind had subsided. I had walked a few blocks away from the hotel and discovered that in the corners of light that fell from the street lamps there appeared to be ash all over the street.

The town was eerily quiet, except for the ash. It sizzled. It sounded like a frying pan on low, scalding bacon. The rising full moon shone red through the smoke. Doomsday? Is this what I've walked into here? Then, I noticed, the ash was moving of its own accord, not blowing in the breeze. The air was solidly still. The ash was alive and not just falling from the sky but flying. I got into the light and stooped down for a closer look. It was not living ash, as I had jolted myself into thinking, but mayflies. Millions of mayflies had hatched in the last hour. They were everywhere. Landing on me. Coursing the air near to every available light source. The ground was littered like parade day with not mounds of confetti, but tiny insect bodies covering every step like a blanket of snow. I reached down and scooped up a handful. They tickled and flew off. There was no way not to step on them. A truck rolled past and left tread marks of death behind him. For the mayflies, this certainly was the bloodiest street in the west. I took pictures which developed much too dark and blurry, nothing that would do the scene justice. Millions might be an understatement; it could have been billions.

I returned to my room and watched TV.

TV is my great escape from reality that in this case gave me comfort with the familiar face of Ben Affleck getting into some kind of trouble and taking me with him out of the room of death. I left all the lights on as I watched and decided to set the clock for the AM. I checked the alarm time and was quite alarmed to find it had already been set for an odd time. 1:05 AM? Who in the world sets an alarm for 1:05 AM? Why is that familiar? Oh yeah, I was born at 1:05 AM! So, that woke me up. I unplugged the clock and set my cell phone alarm for 7:00.

Exhibit P
The Library

I turned up the volume a notch so I could hear Ben Affleck a little better.

I showered with the door open so I could hear the TV, something I rarely do, but that was what I needed at the time to be comfortable. Going into the glass shower cube I remembered, "Didn't they try to drown James Bond, 007 in something like this once? And I don't have a gun to shoot my way out. Probably bulletproof glass anyway. Isn't this how Houdini died in Detroit one Halloween night long ago?" I checked the door to make sure it didn't stick before I turned on the water. Everything was going fine. Water was good. Lights on. Ben Affleck talking. It's safe here. Then I dropped the soap. I reached down to get it and there on the floor outside of the glass stood two naked black feet. I jolted up and there was nobody there. What the hell kind of funhouse illusion was that? I was really wide awake now! I looked down and saw that the bottom of the glass had a smoked mirror on it facing inwards. Those were my own feet that freaked me out. What kind of sicko contractor installs smoked mirror glass on the inside of a shower cube of death? I could have had a heart attack! If somebody did die in that room, that's probably how it happened.

Out of the shower, I realized that on the wall next to the other bed was that mirrored closet door. I looked at the wall that was actually the corner of the building protected from the L shaped room. If that closet went anywhere, it was huge. Pajamaed and slippered, I kneeled up on the other bed and opened the closet. There was a safe inside.

Not just any old safe, but a huge walk-in wall safe. What is this crazy old lady keeping in there? And how did I become the last line of defense before the robbers blast it open with dynamite?

"It's a special room."

You're darn right it is. If it wasn't 83 degrees Fahrenheit outside I'd be sleeping in my car.

But the room had air conditioning and an old oscillating fan that looked one way and then the other and kept things cool enough that psycho killers, ghosts and robbers couldn't get me outside. Besides, it was smoky from the forest fires.

But still, with all this excitement, I couldn't sleep. I had to get that safe open. Destiny called me here. What could the combination be? I tried my date of birth. It didn't open. I tried my social security number. Nope. But I quit after that. With millions of combinations to choose from, whatever was in there, was staying. At least I felt if it were something gruesome that could have killed me, I'd like to think the old lady had years before pulled a Ripley (Alien, Sigourney Weaver) and locked whatever monster existed away in there. Now that I had that idea, I was afraid something might escape instead.

Still struggling with insomnia, I shut off the TV and picked up a book, something I knew. I flipped through a few pages of The Adventures of Huckleberry Finn by Mark Twain. I know I saw Tom Sawyer, but I couldn't find it again. Much like Hotel, it too dealt with corruption and civil rights in the nineteenth century when it was better known as slavery. But there were other lovely moments of freedom felt by the boys on the banks of the Mississippi river and these books are filled with reminiscences of that childhood and its innocence as well as its fears.

I fell asleep with the book in my hand, the light stayed on, and in the morning I was still alive. My hostess informed me that the room I stayed in was once the department stores main office and they kept all the money there. Outside, millions of wispy paper tissue insect bodies littered the ground. Many more had lived than died.

Exhibit Q
Public restroom décor in Billings, Montana - Before Remodel

Exhibit R
Public restroom décor in Billings, Montana - After Remodel

I bought a sandwich and sat beside the Missouri to eat it. Two boys were swimming in the river. A big fish glided past them. They swam to the bridge piling. That was when I thought, this is what Stephen King is going to do to kill his protagonist - one of the boys will get caught in the current and the lone witness on the shore will have to run down the bank and jump in to save him. When he does, his foot will get caught in a branch and he'll be dragged under and drowned. As he fights for breath, he sees the young boy he was trying to save standing on a shallow bank, laughing, because the man fell for his prank. I thought about that scenario real quick and decided 911 would work just fine. They swam to the piling without incident.

I grabbed my camera from the car and framed a picture of the bridge. A man walking past commented to me "There are still places that you can live like Huck Finn, isn't that nice?"

I replied. "It's beautiful."

Exhibit S
Browning, Montana

Exhibit T
Judith Gap, Montana

XVIII

Time Travel

Sent: Saturday, September 1, 2007 1:49 PM
Subject: The Rembis Report - Volume XVIII

My forty-second orbit of the sun is coming to an end tomorrow. In a few hours I will begin my forty-third and a few hours beyond that I will take a great journey with my dear sweet wife Ellen to Manu National Park in Peru.

The first time we traveled to South America we visited Venezuela. The flight from Miami to Caracas was about five hours. Some travelers considered that a long flight, but as we soared over the island of Hispaniola, home to Haiti and the Dominican Republic and later spied the north shore of the continent, I couldn't help but think that the world is an awfully small place. I was amazed that in such a short hop we could be a world away.

A few years later we visited China. The flight from Chicago to Beijing is a thirteen hour and twenty minute non-stop adventure that skirts the arctic circle and weaves through billows of clouds above Alaska's Mt. McKinley (Denali) and Russia's Kamchatka peninsula. When you land in China, again, you are a world away from familiarity and fourteen hours older but since we left at 12:40 PM in Chicago and got to China at 3 PM the next day, we actually catapulted ourselves into the future by 12 hours. Now you could argue that the local time in Chicago is 2 AM, so we didn't really time travel, we just traveled, but take a look at the return trip. Coming back you have an almost thirteen hour trip, (something about the jet stream pushing the airplane makes it go faster) departing at 4:20 PM but you arrive in Chicago on the same day you left at 4:13 PM, a 7 full minutes before you left China. This is time travel. Once again, you could argue that Beijing local time is now 5:13 AM, the next day, which it is, but now you have spent 13 hours in limbo to wind up at exactly the time you started your journey and are 11 hours younger as a result. On the way there you could say that you lost 12 hours so that cancels out the 11 hour differential, but what about the missing hour? Where were we? Did we exist?

When we combine the times traveled to where we actually are now (back in Chicago), total actual travel time is 26 hours and 13 minutes round trip. However, if we set a clock left alone in Chicago, by the time we landed on the return, it should have greeted us with a local time of 6:33 PM the next day (accounting for the turn of the calendar).

This is not what happened. Instead, we existed for an additional 2 hours and 13 minutes to wind up 7 minutes younger. How's that for a paradox? Okay, so what about the 12 hours lost and the 11 hours gained? Doesn't that just leave an hour of missing time? Maybe, it does. That one hour of missing time was stretched into a 2 hour 13 minute interval of actual time for us.

But wait a minute - we're dealing with being 7 minutes ahead of schedule now, let's not change the subject - let's take a look at Beijing Local Time (BLT). Forget about Chicago for a minute. When we left Chicago, the time in Beijing was 12:40 AM the next day, and upon return to Chicago, BLT was 5:13 AM the second day. As far as BLT is concerned, we traveled for 26 hours and 13 minutes, but actual time that had elapsed was 28 hours and 33 minutes.

What does this mean? Somehow it took an extra 2 hours and 20 minutes in China to gain 7 minutes of time in the USA. This means that we are actually, physically older by 2 hours and 13 minutes, and live ahead of actual time.

This is missing time, time that we will never get back. We are living in the future and the rest of you haven't caught up to us yet, unless you take a long plane trip.

I think about time travel a lot.

Einstein proved the possibility if only we had the means to move faster than light, but as you can see I have proved it in another form. Even if it is a form of time travel, I would term this as time drag, simply because it is a way to move back in time and not forward. As you can see it is much more difficult physically, but realistic. As you could see even if you flew eastbound for days on end, you would age drastically to go back in time only a few minutes. You have to endure the punishment of watching the sun rise over and over and the clock not changing and only then will you understand the difficulty of time travel.

To understand time travel according to Albert Einstein find one of the many tutorials to study on the internet and you'll get it.

I once heard a story about a man so superstitious and fearful of Friday the 13th that he flew around the world on Thursday the 12th eastbound from the South Pacific all the way across the ocean to the USA and back across the Atlantic and Indian Oceans to meet the international date line precisely at midnight of Thursday the 12th / Saturday the 14th, so that Friday the 13th could be avoided.

I hope none of you are so superstitious. Trust me, time travel is just not worth the effort. No matter what you decide to miss out on does not mean it won't happen. It also doesn't mean it will happen. Whatever is going to happen, although it may not be predictable is most probably unavoidable.

The Mayans devised a calendar with a cycle of 5,125.36 years that ends on December 21, 2012. There is no way to avoid this date. It is going to happen. This date is going to exist whether you like it or not, and depending upon your level of superstition you might not like it one bit. Some people actually believe the world is going to end on this day. Others take a scientific stance and realize that this is a rare cosmic conjunction that only happens every 5,125.36 years.

The Mayans were pretty advanced with their calculus. In case you are wondering about the astrological ramifications there is a web page that points out that we will actually be at the center of the universe on that day. You understand of course, that I am the center of the universe, it's just going to take 5 more years for everyone else to realize it.

If you are bound to trust the doomsayers there are multiple websites about how your world will come to an end on December 21, 2012, or if you prefer a more personal day of fate, try the Death Clock website.

Of course there are people who don't regard the Mayan Calendar one bit and have their own plans. According to the Zadok Priesthood the second coming of God is most definitely on September 13, 2007, just two weeks away. Their website will give you insights to hundreds of biblical references and a great deal of other verifiable documentation that the world will absolutely, positively end on September 13, 2007 so don't make any plans for next weekend.

September 13 is also Rosh Hashanah and Ramadan. Even Crayola Crayons celebrate Ramadan and Rosh Hashanah.

If you do find it impossible to ignore these harbingers of doom, just remember, you can always take an eastbound flight and do some time travel to avoid the day entirely, and if the world is still here when you get back, you haven't missed a thing. I'll be in Peru that day about to jet back to the USA, hopefully arriving safe at home on the 14th.

What do you think the Zadoks have planned for that day?

XIX

Peru

Sent: Tuesday, October 2, 2007 11:39 PM
Subject: The Rembis Report - Volume XIX

To my dismay, I was informed by my friend, astrophysicist at large Jonathan Rocher, that my theory on time travel was completely inaccurate and he asked me to bring any of my future physics theories to his attention so that they too may be ruled out as well. Jonathan is currently working on constraints on supersymmetric grand unified theories from cosmology and is most interested in The Higgs boson, also known as the God particle, a hypothetical massive scalar elementary particle predicted to exist by the standard model of particle physics, as opposed to gluon, the hypothetical massless, neutral elementary particle believed to mediate the strong interaction that binds quarks together. I am certain that as soon as I am able to explain both gluon and the Higgs boson he will enjoy debunking my theories.

Jonathan was one of our travel companions on our trip to Peru.

Although the flight from Miami to Lima was just over 5 hours, for me, it may as well have been twenty. I just can't sit still that long, so once again, it felt like time travel. Or perhaps I was just feeling the ill-effects of gluon or the Higgs boson.

Touching down to wait for yet another plane to Cuzco was simply a tease before that final hour of flight to the Andes. When we did get to Cuzco, we were greeted by a warmhearted city eager to share coca tea, carved Inca-style trinkets, and reams of brightly woven alpaca. The city is an auspicious clean grid work of masonry. Our hotel was remodeled from an original residence built about 600 years ago with walls four feet thick. The city bustles. Every conveyance and convenience you expect from a modern metropolis is available and ready for consumption, yet the locals resonate an old world charm that prides itself on the fullness of its dual heritage, both the native Inca and the adopted Spanish influence. They are as proud of the stone steps and pathways of their ancestral Incan architecture as they are of the grand Catholic churches and cathedrals that adorn every corner of the city. There are no fewer than a dozen parishes within a few blocks of the city center, all of them magnificent examples of 16th century workmanship. Inside, photographs are not allowed and solemn tours are conducted around parishioners kneeling in prayer. On the street, locals will pose for photos for only a Sol (about 33 cents) and you wind up with a great National Geographic style that screams *PERU!*

After a day in Cusco, we met our guide, Ronnie Collado, Jungle Specialist. No kidding, that is his title, and it fits him perfectly. He spotted dozens of animals for us and explained how they lived and what we were hearing. There are a lot of sounds in the jungle. The howler monkey is about the creepiest thing you could ever hear outside of a horror movie. I made some videos of otters and a giant tapir but did not include it here because I am only now learning to edit film on a computer and upload it. I'll have a small clip for you to watch next month. Ronnie introduced us to our other travel companions, Raoul and Daphne, from California, and we all drove out to the Cloud Forest together.

The tiny minivan rocked and tumbled along the rutted dirt road from Cuzco's 11,000 foot elevation and took us over a pass near 13,000 feet before sloping down toward the cloud forest at 5,500 feet about 200 kilometers away. Mileage is measured metrically in Peru and since I am metrically challenged, I'll let you do the math, if you wish. The Andes in this region are remote but by no means uninhabited. There is village upon village and abundant farming on the slopes. The crops are planted and harvested not always on structured plateaus, but most times, are simply growing straight up a hill at a 45 - 60 degree angle. One woman we spotted was hoeing or harvesting some vegetables and digging her knees into the hill, working nearly upright, with one baby on her back and another in her belly. We passed many shepherds leading their flocks of sheep and sometimes cattle along the highway and when we reached the last major town before the cloud forest, European clothing was scant compared to the vibrant styles of the Andean culture. A rainbow of people poured through this town, most wearing traditional garments and adorned with wide brimmed Chullo hats.

Soon the high plains gave way to the forest and the clouds rolled in. Curious about the cloud forest, I asked Ronnie "Is it always cloudy?" wondering if we just caught it on a particularly cloudy day or if most times the jungle around us was bathed in sunlight.

He told me "Yes. Always."

This dense jungle sometimes gives way to massive outcroppings and towering waterfalls and every kilometer the road gets muddier and we squeeze past cargo trucks wedged between them and a 3,000 foot cliff. One wrong move and . . .well, we didn't have that kind of excitement.

At the Cock of the Rock Lodge, we watched spider monkeys frolic and eat bananas. The Cock of the Rock is Peru's national bird, and this is one of the few places you can see it. It's loud and red and something like a squat rooster. Hummingbirds flitted about the lodge as well and in the morning we moved on another 80 kilometers to the river.

Rio Madre de Dios (The Mother of God River) is a shallow waterway peppered with a gauntlet of massive ancient trees that have succumbed to landslides and spring floods. Kapok and ironwoods build the canopy that gives life to a nearly impenetrable forest below. There are no roads or trails here. Only the river that leads us to Boca Manu another 90 kilometers away. As the crane flies, it may only be 50 kilometers, but the river twists and turns and heads in every direction but straight ahead, so reaching Boca Manu and the next camp takes all day. We see more monkeys and many birds on this stretch.

In Boca Manu we purchase the last 12 bottles of Cusquena Cerveza (Beer) in the entire town. Oh, what a grand evening. Our huts sit in a glen near the airstrip. Fireflies rival the stars above and insects crank out a deafening chorus until the temperature drops to about 75 F. Most of the day the thermometer hovers near 90 F.

A plane lands on the airstrip this morning introducing us to Jonathan and his bride-to-be, Alice, who are visiting from Texas. We return to the river and both Daphne and I misstep and find ourselves glued in the mud. I fare better than her because I keep my boots tied securely at all times. I think she had flip flops that she almost couldn't find. That was probably the worst of our troubles this trip aside from the mosquito bites.

Exhibit U
Citizens of Cuzco, Peru model traditional garb for tourists

At this point, we are at the terminus of the Manu river and head upstream into the heart of Manu National Park. Our destination now is another twisting journey of 110 kilometers. This is far from everywhere. Very far. But with Abel at the bow and Wilson at the stern we are confident in reaching our destination and avoiding disaster.

In Venezuela, Ellen and I traveled up the Rio Parucito (Parasite River) to Mosquito Creek. It was also far from everywhere and by comparison, much more remote and dangerous. On that trip we were far off the grid and not traveling through a monitored area like a national park. Caiman and piranha were abundant. Here, in Manu, we felt less in danger, yet still very much alive. Camping in a hut with a mattress is far preferable to just hanging the mosquito netting over the hammock and wishing each other luck. "See you in the morning. I hope."

Manu is a relatively safe jungle adventure and there were plenty of travelers visiting from all over the world even in their 50's and 60's and perhaps older yet. In Venezuela, we met a girl for whom we were the only white people she had ever seen. In the Manu, this is not the case. The Machiguenga tribe is another three hours upstream from where we stopped but we did meet a Machiguenga family across the river who moved closer to civilization and carved bows and arrows and offered bead jewelry for sale. I was hoping to have some kind of unique experience, meeting these people, as we did in Venezuela, but these gaunt Machiguengas do business with currency, not T-shirts or other trade goods. They are not dressed like savages but in soccer attire branded by LG, the company that makes TVs and cell phones.

Ronnie explained to us that the Peruvian government has set up safeguards to protect indigenous tribes from invasion, primarily for the sake of maintaining a cultural heritage that is untainted by missionary work. They record every person entering the jungle and their purpose for being there to ensure the sanctity of the wildlife and the rainforest. Mahogany and other hardwoods in Peru are under government control and price ceilings have been placed on these items making a plank of desirable wood virtually worthless so that they may not be harvested, thus protecting the forest for future generations and for the land itself. The Machiguengas and many other tribes hidden deep within the interior do not welcome visitors or infringement on their society and have successfully lobbied the Peruvian government to place restrictions on missionary work so that they are left undisturbed. If a tribal member wishes to leave, they may, but getting in to see these people is an entirely different and difficult adventure to fulfill.

We move on to the Manu Wildlife Center to witness flocks of macaws, parakeets, and parrots that swarm over the clay clicks by the hundreds. They eat the clay to aid digestion of the toxins in the fruit that make up their primary diet. So too, does the tapir, a docile lumbering beast, like a hippo or manatee on land with a short elephantine snout, it warily approaches the clay lick at night to partake of the minerals it also needs to survive. Although it is as large as a refrigerator, it is nearly blind and skittish, afraid of sounds in the distance. We survey him from a blind and maintain deft silence. He eats and slurps noisily and looks around for danger. The bright lights splayed upon him have no effect, and something in the brush to our right rustles, forcing the tapir to bolt away through the foot-deep mud. We wait ten minutes and he returns to eat again. Large and ugly by most definitions, I found the tapir to be the most beautiful and innocent of animals, simply trying to get along in his tropic home undisturbed.

So it is with the native tribes we would never meet. What may be the most beautiful of life we may never see, whether hidden in a forest, high atop a mountain, or deep in the ocean depths.

Scientists searching for answers may witness such wonders while other visitors, namely missionaries, may not recognize these cultures as beauty, but blasphemy. They have a simpler purpose that they wholeheartedly believe in - to convert people and save souls - that is really what they think they are doing. The New Tribes Mission touts this tagline "...reaching new tribes until the last tribe has been reached."

It is evident that mankind has suffered greater cultural losses in the name of religion than in the name of science and most notably in language; one is said to be lost completely every two weeks. On this trip, we studied Spanish beforehand and had our basic phrases ready for typical exchanges, but most of the time English was quite sufficient and the American dollar was welcomed as currency. The invasion of the outside world continues and just as the Conquistadors destroyed the Incan temples and built their Cathedrals atop the ruins, even now that religious terrorism slowly spreads over time and distance and shocks me when I learn the names of the Machiguengas who have left the tribe to set up shop downstream; Carlos and his son, Christian.

I also learned that those few people who do interact with missionaries, at least in this region, take advantage of them and change their religions to suit their guests at that moment. I incorporated this knowledge into my latest audition for the online show The Interior. You can watch the first 10 episodes online right now. Each episode is only about 5 minutes long, but it is intriguing. The show is about missionaries in the South American Amazon. I auditioned for the role of Angel and you can watch my audition on YouTube. I filmed it in Manu.

At the end of the audition, because I am new at film editing, I inadvertently placed an extra 20 seconds of footage featuring the morning cries of the howler monkey that hung out in the trees above our camp. We wondered about stranger and larger unseen creatures that may exist, like dinosaurs or a large bipedal similar to Bigfoot, but Ronnie assured us that Sasquatchamente does not exist.

At the end of our trip we brought home luggage filled with dirty laundry, obviously fouled to the nth degree by either gluon or Higgs boson, laundry that may never be completely clean no matter how much detergent or bleach we apply. If only we could have called on The Panty Fairy, a character now being brought to life with the help of one of my BESTest friends Jill Ginter, who is now Jillian Kinsman. See her in the Panty Fairy commercial on YouTube.

Finally, thank you all for taking the time to read The Rembis Report and watch for next month's edition when I will include the tapir footage.

Watch out for those gluons, they can ruin a shirt.

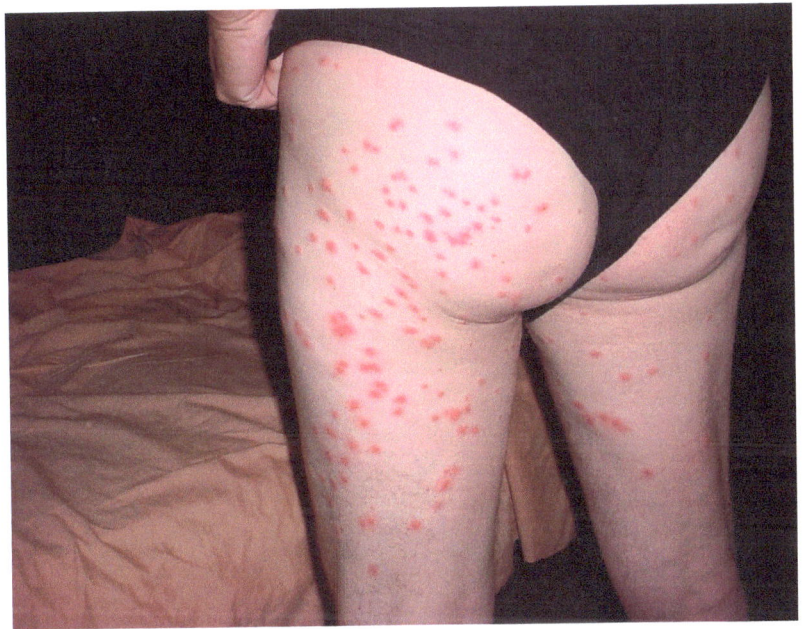

Exhibit V
The Manu

XX

Halloween in Billings

Sent: Thursday, November 1, 2007 4:45 PM
Subject: The Rembis Report - Volume XX

Now, we wait.
The pumpkins are carved. The candy sits in a pile. The leaves have been brushed off the steps. It is light out and the trick-or-treaters will not arrive until a few hours from now. If you recall, last year, high on the hill in Livingston we had sleet and not one single goblin braved the cold to visit. This year, we are in a more residential area in Billings and expect to have some type of parade. I know there are children in the neighborhood.

We live on a quiet street, only a block long. A place where you can calmly walk your dog or ride a bicycle without a car whizzing past, not every minute anyway. Most drivers here maintain a stoic amble and coast to a stop. Very few drive with a demonic edge.

Now that so many leaves have dropped, from our front lawn you can see the rimrock. In the sunset an earthy pastel hue glows under a milky blue sky. The crescent moon will rise over the rim a few hours from now, probably after the beggars have retreated.

The sun sets and about a dozen little ghouls show up wanting treats. They come in a tiny pack, all costumed like skeletons or killers.

In years past I would greet them as a Werewolf or a New Years Partygoer telling them they were late. This year I was going to put on my plain-collar shirt and pose as a Catholic Priest, but my dear sweet wife, Ellen, said that would be too scary. So tonight, I opted for the Headless Lumberjack, pulling my flannel shirt up over my head and raising an axe up in the air.

I missed that first round of kids and waited for the next. An hour later. I am still waiting. They are walking down the street on the corner, but not turning down here. Half the lights on our block are on. There is candy and houses are frightfully decorated, but nobody comes. The man across the street sits on his stoop and smokes a cigarette. He looks both ways, walks to the center of the street and shakes his head sadly.

Why do we not have trick-or-treaters? Neighbors warned us that there would not be many. They were right. Here it is, pitch black, the candles in the Jack O'Lanterns are vaporizing and moonlight lingers on the rimrock. Soon, it will be too late for reasonable parents to have their children out knocking on doors and most certainly, there will be no one. A dog barks on the next block, so there must be somebody walking by over there. I take my dog, Mama, for a walk around the block. On our own street, more than half the porch lights are on and on the next block, almost every light is on, and on the adjacent street, other hovels glow brightly awaiting the deserted streets where not one child walks. Halloween is lonely here this year.

Exhibit W
Trick or Treat

Exhibit X
Jack O'Lanterns

Now I know how the Grinch must have felt when he stole Christmas and nobody cared. What's wrong with those Whos down in Whoville? *"It came without presents, it came without tags! It came without packages, boxes or bags!"7* How utterly dreadful. Then, tonight, the reverse - we waited with piles of candy and frightful scares to make the evening complete - and nothing. One of the few children who did show up told his mother "His head's under his shirt."

Oh, youth, rotten little youth. How dare you defy Halloween. May we show you how the axe works?

Maybe next year. Tonight, crisp and cool, beautiful and still, not even a leaf rustles. The howling winds are far away. We extinguish the candles and the Jack O'Lanterns dim.

We sleep.

I got the most wonderful notice for my audition on YouTube. Christian Badami, one of the stars of The Interior, the show which the audition is for, wrote quite a nice review. I hope you'll read it. From there you can also link to his YouTube page and see some of his stagecraft, or check out my favorites and watch commercials starring my BESTest friends Jill Ginter and Darla Delgado.

By the way, if you still want to celebrate Halloween, (I know I do), you can catch Darla and my friend Julia Denton Francis in this little fright-fest that went straight to video release - The Woods Have Eyes.

You can read the review
and if it's scary to you,
add it to your queue,
too.

That was supposed to rhyme.

And if you think that's frightening, I'd like to know who went to see Vampire Biker Babes, starring another of my BESTest Friends, Georgia Chris and my former scene partner, Venue Actors Studio alumni Junia Dawn. I know the premiere was last weekend, so somebody had to see it. Please send me a review!

Finally, if you want to see something you probably won't find anywhere but the internet, take a look at Dan Diaz' latest project, The Isles of Tyrannos, created by Matt Guercia at Rock Noise Animation. They just posted the first episode and the second is right behind it. Dan plays Mog, a very successful prehistoric spearfisherman. Watch if you dare. I am still reeling.

That's all the news that's fit to print, for now. Watch what you can and write those reviews. Actors love feedback.

Take Care, Mike

XXI

Heroes

Sent: Sunday, December 02, 2007 2:30 AM
Subject: The Rembis Report - Volume XXI

Jeff Mulvaney wrote on the dry erase board "Duffy is my hero" in response to Chris Duffy's 15.5% increase in revenue this week. In our sales office, Jeff and Duff are pals and tease each other's performance relentlessly. Jeff's blurb of heroism was meant, of course, as a mockery. He did not really consider Duffy a hero, and if he had, well, I suppose that would mean that Jeff's standards are pretty low.

What is a hero? You hear this term uttered almost daily on the news. Heroes die in foreign wars or battle for the underprivileged. That is our typical definition of a hero. I was thumbing through an appointment book for 2008 while I waited my turn to meet a customer yesterday. In the upper right hand margin on every page there are quotes from famous or well-known people as well as some by Unknown authors. Quotes from Voltaire to Stephen King to John Lennon to Tom Brokaw and one from Dr. Martin Luther King,

Jr. adorns the week of March 17 to 23 (St. Patrick's Day to Easter this year) *"If a man hasn't discovered something that he would die for, he isn't fit to live."*[8]

That's pretty harsh. Did MLK really say that? If he did, it's likely that he meant it. Just reading and absorbing those words makes one ask of themselves, what would I die for? My answer is that I don't know. I don't want to go. Life is good. No matter how difficult it gets, I'll take the pain of life over the mystery of death any day of the week. That's easy to say when your life isn't so hard. I don't do much of anything terribly death-defying, other than driving incessantly, so if that qualifies, I suppose being behind the wheel is something that I routinely risk my life for. But this is not heroic.

I'd suppose that the maxim of my heroism lies in animal rescue. I can't pass an injured animal without administering aid. I've picked up birds or cats or turtles to get them out of the roads. During the hurricanes that swept over Florida a few years ago, Ellen and I rescued several baby squirrels whose nests fell from the trees.

We sent them to rehabilitation and as soon as they were old enough to break their addiction for hand-feeding they were released safely into the wild, time served, probation suspended. Is that a heroic act? Maybe if you're a squirrel, it is.

The fact is that not everybody becomes a hero, and some people never get to meet one, so we must create our own, by personal definition.

Spiderman is a hero. Not just any hero, but a Superhero! That means he's really good at it. He fights guys like Doctor Octopus and Mysterio, whose sole purpose is to exploit in the name of selfishness, while Spidey lives a life of repentance by vengeance for the death of his Uncle Ben. (No, not the rice guy, keep up, will you?) Stan Lee's Spiderman became a hero because he had to. His own guilt is what led him on a path of righteousness. Had he stopped the first bad guy when he had the chance, would he have become morally indebted

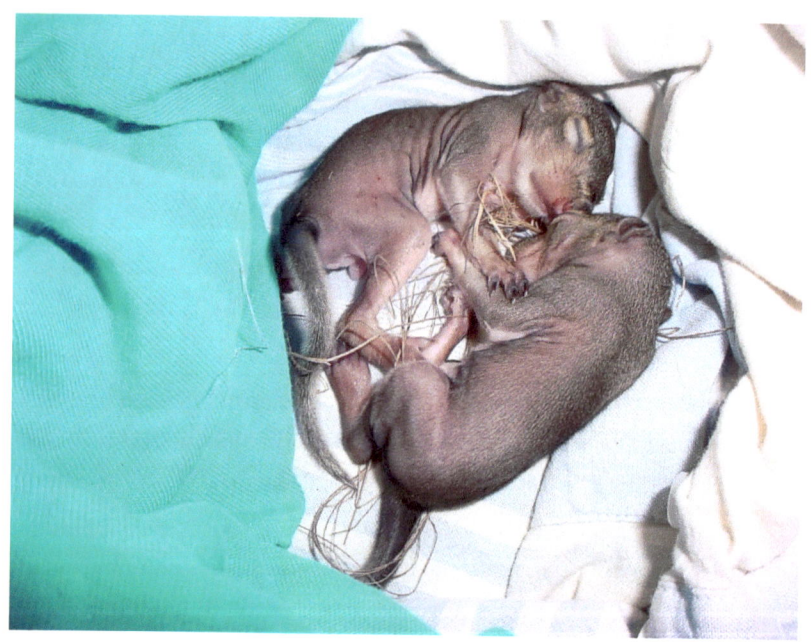

Exhibit Y
Baby Squirrels

to society to fight in the name of justice? Since the story is already written, there is no way to say for sure. Only Stan Lee could answer that one.

It seems that everybody has a Superhero they admire. I always loved Spiderman, and don't exactly know why. Maybe it was the animal morphism of being part arachnid with unique powers, like web-slinging and soaring over the rooftops of the city. Maybe it was the anonymity, or perhaps the costume itself. Although there was no cape, it made a great pair of pajamas that doubled as underwear in second grade, and we all know how comfortable it is to walk around all day in your pajamas. Delving deeper into my own psyche, I may not discover why, but I do not believe understanding it is at all necessary to enjoy having Spiderman as my favorite.

Shortly after I purchased my Mustang, I went to Hardees for lunch and ordered one of those meals where you get a toy. I did this specifically for the toy: a Spiderman-head antenna fob. It was mounted ceremoniously on my antenna and I drove around under Spidey's watchful eye for five years. Then, one morning in Great Falls, when I emerged from my hotel room he was gone. Somebody stole my Spiderman fob. It was devastating. We drove thousands of miles together, Spidey and I. He even rode cross country with Chris Pio when he took my car from Florida to Montana, braving tornado stricken Tennessee and the loathsome speed traps of rural Wyoming. To have that naked antenna wobbling about was crushing, especially since I knew it was a theft that would never be solved.

I would not, however, admit defeat - HELL NO! I logged on to eBay and found another one and a week later, Spider Man 2 and I were cruising the blacktop of Montana once more. That was last year. But just this week, tragedy struck again.

On Interstate 90 westbound at the Zoo Drive exit in Billings, a howling 70 MPH gust of wind hurled a tumbleweed at my car. Tumbleweeds are common in the western plains, the biggest are usually globes of baby's breath a yard wide that have snapped off their stems to become silent wanderers. They are generally harmless. They bounce away and across the road. This one was huge, at least a four-footer. I could see it looming ahead of us. The paint job on my Mustang is not something I am particularly fond of, so I don't worry a bit about scratches of any kind. The pockmarks it bears and those to come I simply consider battle scars of a road warrior. The collision course was evident. I thought I might just get past it, and slamming on the brakes for a tumbleweed with cars directly behind me was not something I would do to ensure the integrity of a paint job I cared nothing about. So there we were - me and Spidey against a rogue tumbleweed. It could not have hit the antenna more dead-on. There was a THWACKKKKKKKK! and the tumbleweed rolled over the car to be devoured by the vehicle behind me. I looked up to see my antenna whipping about furiously. Spidey was gone. He sacrificed himself to save me. I thought for a moment about stopping on that icy patch of road to go and find him, but as nice as people are in Montana, if I did that, there would soon be five people stopping to see if I was okay there on the side of the road and it would have caused an accident. So I left Spiderman 2 to bask in immortality and I will hold that grand memory forever.

Memories like this one are good. Even if it is silly, and probably because it is very silly, it is good. I have a good memory. I remember almost everything about particular instances, little scenes from my life that I recall over and over again. Mostly, I like to think about good things, funny episodes or oddly ironic events and these experiences create the whole of my being and have crafted me into who I am, and I can't help thinking about it. Sometimes I feel as if I am in a constant state of reminiscence.

Just as we see the transformation of Peter Parker into Spider-man, we can all look back on our lives and see how tiny events have shaped us into who we are now. Sometimes events are merely chapters of a story that ends years later. You don't recognize it at the time, but you record that event and hold onto the memory until you can use it or understand what happened to begin with.

When we had an art gallery in Spokane in 1993, there was an Irish Pub around the corner and once in a while, I stopped for a pint. Right next door was a vacant facade with an Evel Knievel jacket hanging in the window. Next to it was a painting of Evel and some other Evel memorabilia with a sign that said something like *"Evel Knievel and D.A.R.E. keeps kids off drugs."* The facade wasn't part of any downtown establishment or related to anything except what I have just described. It was just there and I never knew why. About a week before we closed the gallery, I was in the pub having a beer before going home. One man who I would see at the bar occasionally was there. I think he drank water or pop. We nodded and said "Hello" to one another in mutual recognition as he said goodbye to the barkeep. We never had a single conversation. That day, the last time I went to that pub, I happened to ask the barkeep about the window full of curios next door that paid tribute to Evel Knievel. The barkeep told me "They're his. He just puts them on display."

"Who?"

"Evel Knievel."

"You know him?"

"You were just talking to him." he replied as if I should have known.

At this point in the story, I suppose that if you don't know who Evel Knievel is you may not be American. For those out of touch with recent American folklore and mainstream media, he is touted as a true hero, sometimes, a superhero. He died yesterday. Not fighting any super-villain, but of an illness his mortal frame could not defeat.

A few years ago, when we lived in Clearwater, my acting coach Corinne Broskette, told me that she saw him at a gas station in Pinellas Park and he was signing autographs for some children.

"Why was he signing autographs at a gas station? I asked.

"He was getting gas."

Of course, I should have known that.

Some days later, as Spiderman (the original one) and I were crossing the Bayside Bridge toward 49th street, a white crew cab truck creeped up alongside the Mustang. I looked in the rear view mirror and noticed an odd custom grill coming into focus. The truck stayed close to me across the length of the bridge, about two miles. In the center of the grill were two unmistakable initials - EK. Who does that to their vehicle? There were thin blue stripes with red stars inside that adorned the hood and fenders and at the wheel an old man with glasses on and wild white hair. Instantly, I knew it was Evel Knievel, so I waved and saluted. I can't say that he smiled, but he did wave and salute back. As he passed me, I was positive of the identification by his license plate that read EVEL with a number. That was great.

Maybe you have to have been a kid with an Evel Knievel lunch box at one time to truly appreciate it. But there I was, face to face, cruising alongside a real American Hero. His infamous legacy is one without equal. He was a daredevil that did something different only because he had a desire to do it. Evel was as self made as a man could be. He was human and at the same time seemingly indestructible. As kids we jumped our bicycles over small mounds of dirt and ramps to be just like him. He always did what he said he was going to do - he jumped, hell or high water, he jumped. Over 300 times, just for the thrill of it. Once in a while he crashed and broke every bone in his body or wound up in a coma. Somehow this became admirable. Why? Because he did it. Something that nobody else was doing, Evel

Knievel did it. He was so incredible that they turned him into a GI Joe-type action figure. He wore a one of a kind outfit and a cape.

Spidey

Other than Superman and Dracula the only real life guys who ever got away with wearing a cape were Elvis Presley, Liberace and James Brown and they most likely got the idea from Evel. I mean, that takes guts to wear a cape in public. Think about it.

Tom Thompson once told me "You're the only person I know who wears saddle shoes yet somehow you're able to pull it off. They look normal on you." Damn if I didn't feel like a hero.

So now I understand why I almost met Evel so long ago in Spokane and then again on the road years later. My supposition is that this was fate. That I would have a reason to correlate my loss of Spider Man 2 and tie it into the demise of Evel Knievel in order to write this essay. In a twisted way, it all makes sense.

Another man who had a way of making sense out of life was my recently departed father-in-law Raymond Wittek. I knew Ray for 20 years and as this farewell attests he truly was a wonderful man. He was married to Evelyn for over 50 years. They raised four kids and I married their youngest daughter, Ellen, who considers him her personal hero. He was a reporter for the Staten Island Advance and covered numerous groundbreaking stories over a 40 year career. He was a talented painter and our walls carry some of his best and most precious work. Most of all, he made friends, which is about the best thing you can do with your life if you're not a superhero. What could make more sense than that?

Some of my friends have been busy. Jonathan Rocher sent us more pictures of our trip to Manu. I am particularly fond of the aerial photo of the runway he took just before landing in the jungle. I am a tiny dot that even I can not find in that picture, standing beside the runway watching the plane approach. Jonathan has a fantastic camera and took some great shots. But if still photos don't do it for you, please watch the first installment of our Peruvian Jungle Adventure on YouTube. This is a video I shot and you'll notice some of Jonathan's subjects brought to life. I am not a professional videographer or film editor and I am certain this 8 minutes of film will prove that. But it was fun. Watch for the giant otters.

Time for a shameless plug. It's Christmastime folks, and you know what that means, it may be quite possible you're going to shop. If that is indeed the case, please check out the websites brought to us by Venue alumni Missy Escribano and BESTest friend Jillian Ginter Kinsman (Which last name should we be using Jill?)

If you can't find what you're looking for here, shop somewhere else.

Was that okay? Should I do another take? Convincing? Not sure I was feeling it.

Maybe I should try it with a cape.

Merry Christmas, Happy Hanukkah and have a wild Kwanzaa. See you next year!

XXII

Christmas

Sent: Wednesday, January 02, 2008 2:38 AM
Subject: The Rembis Report - Volume XXII

I'm not turning out the Christmas lights. Not yet. I took down the tree this weekend, but the outside lights, the twinkling white icicles, the large colored bulbs along the front porch trellis and the netted lights on the wall fashioned into the shape of a tree with a bright snowflake star on top are staying. Maybe only a few more days, but right now, I like the way they look so Christmas time will last a few days longer.

We did survey many of our neighborhoods here in Billings for their displays. Any light at all was a cheerful addition to the season, I felt, because so many people did not put up lights. In other places, it seems that in years past displays were much more prevalent. Salt Lake City was insanely illuminated when we lived there. A baby Jesus on every lawn.

There was one particular display in SLC that was tucked away in an old neighborhood that had weathered the influx of industrialization and had only a few homes standing among the warehouses. As I recall, it was only a block or two from State street, alone on an otherwise deserted pathway. Of course, being the only house, the decorations blazed from afar. This little display was tended to lovingly. A few of the ornaments moved slightly, like dolls with candles and carousels with stuffed animals. Lights strung around the fenced yard showered the fixtures of Santa and reindeer in a rainbow. These were ancient icons from the early days of plastic snowmen lit with 100 watt bulbs in their bellies, a manger scene whose wise men and camels were extremely weathered, but whose painted eyes still stared down into the crib. Snoopy and Woodstock skated the same figure eight on a tiny frozen birdbath. Toy soldiers and nutcrackers guarded the front porch. Brightly lit M&M bulbs were being strung by their larger siblings Plain and Peanut. This display was so unique and lost in it's own simplicity, we visited it for three years in a row. It never changed, as well as we could remember. And we never took a picture. The last time I saw it was 1998. But if I went back to Salt Lake at Christmas, I'll bet you I could find it, as long as that person is still there and decorating, I think I'd know the street.

It's getting harder to find those gracefully established displays. Where I grew up, in Detroit, we always drove along Outer Drive in Dearborn and Dearborn Heights certain to find Rudolph the Red-Nosed Reindeer leading Santa's sleigh on top of one particular house. Farther out, near Livonia, I think, we would visit Santa's workshop at one place that was decorated with giant candy canes along the walkway and a white haired Mrs. Claus would greet us and we would sometimes meet with Santa himself. This was great fun for my younger siblings, but I knew it wasn't the real Santa Claus. I had met the real Santa Claus when I was five at the Christmas Carnival in Cobo Hall.

The Christmas Carnival was a great place to go for a little kid whose parents wanted them to get tired. It was hot and noisy and looked something like Whoville. There were games where you threw styrofoam snowballs and ring tosses and water guns that filled exploding balloons. Stuffed animal prizes and tons of sticky candy and frozen Coca-Cola. Giant pretzels. Elves walking around. Santa's sleigh. And in a hay laden pen with a line going what must have been a mile, reindeer, real reindeer with little bells on, and you could pet them. Then the longest line of all led to the giant plywood cutout that had two words I could actually read by myself with no help from anybody - "Santa's Castle." He was in there, really in there! Not like the Santa at the mall you could see from a mile away, but like a rock star or a really cool politician you just don't get to meet unless you're really special. So we stood in line. We waited a long time. My mom knew how important it was to me that if Santa Claus came all the way to Detroit in 1969, right after the race riots of 1967, that I better get in there and let him know how much I appreciate that gesture. I mean, if I didn't happen to live in Detroit at the time, I certainly wouldn't have gone there for any reason. Sure we had a great baseball team, but come on, they played in other cities.

Finally, my turn came. A one on one meeting with Mr. C. I was going to tell him everything I wanted that Christmas. I prepared a list. Even memorized it. Santa Claus, in the flesh, right here in Detroit, Michigan, USA, and I was going to meet him. I turned the corner and I saw him sitting there on a huge gold and red velvet throne. He wasn't quite what I expected. I was thinking "Well, he's kind of skinny, not the jolly old elf I was thinking and something about him is definitely diffe- wait a minute! He's black!"

But he greeted me with a big "Ho, ho, ho! Merry Christmas Michael!" And that's when I learned the unshakable truth about Christmas, the real Santa Claus is a black man, and I met him.

He looked a lot like this gentleman here.

Suddenly I had the facts. I know he was the real Santa Claus because everything I told him I wanted that year, I got. Even at that young age, when I would see white actors playing Santa Claus on TV or in other stores, I knew they were phonies and the product of the White Christmas conspiracy. This year, my prayers were answered and Santa Claus somehow, I don't know how, got in touch with one of my BESTest friends and (probably because I'm a good boy) I got a new Spiderman fob for my antenna! Thanks Annette, I didn't know you were so tight with the man, that's so cool. I guess he remembers me.

If you haven't taken your decorations down yet, don't worry, and don't hurry. Christmas is good for everyone and New Year's Eve never hurt anyone too bad either. Mama Dog is still celebrating.

Happy New Year 2008! Be Good!

Black Santa

Mama Dog

XXIII

Another New Adventure

Sent: Thursday, January 31, 2008 5:12 PM
Subject: The Rembis Report - Volume XXIII

We are yet again on the verge of a new existence. Not the whole world, just mine and Ellen's. In a month or so we will journey to another new beginning, this time in Austin Texas to unfold the pages on the next chapter of our lives. I know it confuses people more than anything else about the way we live, appearing to move about as gypsies while simultaneously maintaining a grounded and structured work ethic and home life. Drives some folks crazy that we can do this. Most people don't live this way. The majority (of people in the world) live only a few miles from the place they grew up and physically close to blood relatives their entire lives. I have always said that I am not a tree. I'm more like a leaf that floats on whatever soft breezes carry me in a happy direction.

"*Success seems to be connected with action. Successful people keep moving. They make mistakes, but they don't quit."* ~Conrad Hilton[9] This is the motto or mission statement on my BESTest friend Darla Delgado's Myspace page. Mine is simpler and more subtle: *"Witnessing Stupidity since 1964."*

One person asked me if moving to Montana was a mistake and my answer is no, it's an adventure. That's what life is all about. Trying new things, seeing what's out there. If I didn't bring you a first hand account of what Montana is really like, who would? But now it's on to Texas, for even greater adventures, and hopefully, more auditions. I auditioned for one movie and four plays in the last two years and was cast just one time. Even at that, no bio appeared in the program, which doesn't happen here. Acting and being on TV is treated as a privilege here, not a job to get paid for. A Billings production company asked me once if I would have an issue portraying a recovering addict for a drug and alcohol rehabilitation facility.

"Will I have to go through rehab?" I asked.

"No, but people will recognize you on the street and think that you did because they don't realize that the people on TV are actors."

Another prime example of why Montana is no place for an actor is that I just got a call in response to my submission to ABC's casting for The Mole, a reality show, and when it was discovered that I was based in Montana, the invitation was immediately rescinded. It's like when I was younger and had to stop telling people I was from Detroit. They always thought I could help fix their cars. For whatever reason, people attach stigmas to places and pass judgments quickly just because of where you are from and there's nothing you can do about it. For all I know the casting director has been reading forwarded Rembis Reports and decided to cross Montana off the application list because of everything he's heard about it. If that is indeed the case, I have just proved the existence of karma. It didn't matter that I could make it to the East side of Manhattan next week for an audition, he just told me to forward my info to the casting office in Los Angeles. Maybe it's a nice way to *"Just say NO"* to Montana.

I spoke with my agent in Absarokee yesterday who told me that the Screen Actors Guild in Seattle told her that Montana would never get any SAG affiliations because there is no industry here. Not a lot of encouragement to stick around.

So why Austin? Why not LA or New York where the only time anyone expects to hear the word Montana is with Hannah placed before it?

Austin was recently rated as the Best Place to Make Movies this year.

Just down the road in Houston they ranked 10th. Good news for my friends in Orlando, your town just went from unranked to 5th place!

We started our research a few months ago and found that of the top ten at that time, when Austin ranked 4th, it turned out to have everything else we needed in the way of affordability and work potential. We did further research, hopped on a plane and when we got down there, everything seemed to feel like it was falling into place so we bought a house.

It is as scary as it is comforting. I always like going someplace new. When I used to hitchhike, the best thing about it was not knowing exactly where you might be in a few hours or the next day or who you might meet. It is that same mystery that excites me again. I see fantastic potential and opportunity before us and stories to tell of where I've been that will intrigue those I have yet to meet.

Saying goodbye to Montana will not be difficult as I have done it twice before, to move once to Baltimore and years later to Florida. Yes, we've been around, and we plan to go further. The next Rembis Report may be delayed a few days after we actually arrive in Austin, or it may be written on the road, or quite possibly, moments before departure, but fear not, it will be written. We'll pack up the cats and Mama Dog and load up a rental truck and go. We'll drive safely, sticking to major roads and hope for mild weather and sunny days. As for hitchhikers, I doubt we'll have room, especially if he looks anything like this. I mean, we love zebras, but they really should ride on the bus.

One of my friends asked me this about last month's R.R.: *"You didn't really meet a black Santa Claus, did you?"*

I promise, every word of the Rembis Report is 100% true. I save fiction for my screenplays.

Until next time, watch for my latest online auditions on YouTube. Later, Mike

Exhibit Z
Zebra

XXIIIa

Addendum

Sent: Thursday, January 31, 2008 8:34 PM
Subject: The Rembis Report - Volume XXIII Addendum

Addendum? Bet you never thought you'd see that, did you? I know, it surprised me too.

When proofing this report, my dear sweet wife Ellen noticed that the date on the article I sent you about Austin was February 2, 2004.

"WHAT!!!!!!!!!!!!!! How can that be?"

Well, Austin was a great place for filming in 2003 and it started quite a trend, so . . . .

"But I just saw it on the news! On TV! They said it on TV so it must be true!"

Yes, they did, and Austin is, as of January 28, 2008 at the top of the annual list again.

"Whew! I just bought a house."

Right. Can you shut up now so I can finish?

"Go ahead."

Anyway, that's the good news. The bad news is that Orlando is not on the current list. But don't feel bad. Neither is Los Angeles.

From The Response File
Volume XXIII addendum

Received: Wednesday, February 13, 2008 6:18 AM

Having been part of the movement known to our family as the Great Smithorbob Northern Migration of 2007, to be followed 7 months later by the Smithorbob Florida or Bust, I know just how you feel with the anticipation and excitement of moving. It's the whole idea that anything can happen and usually does even with the best of planning. We went north to Virginia and 7 months later turned around and came right back...and even through both ways moving were filled with happiness but also bittersweet at the same time--filled with the promise of (Virginia) "we're going to love our new neighbors and we'll have loads of friends and it will be like a 1950's suburb"....to the return (Florida) of "this time I won't waste one single moment of sunshine no matter what and enjoy every opportunity that comes around" but do not envy you having to deal with 1. the DMV and 2. utilities. I have no words to really describe the horridness of customer UNservice and mass confusion caused by simply moving back to where you were..."but I just want the same service I had....it's all the same, we just came back..." and the poor post office could not keep up. It was months before we stopped getting mail with that pleasant yellow sticker on the bottom...I inadvertently filled out the wrong form when returning, so instead of canceling the mail forward I filled out a new one, and our mail was caught in a loop going from one post office in Virginia to Florida, and never actually making it out of anyone's bag to find out where we were. And I don't regret our moves at all, it's all dominoes and karma, and one phase of our life feeds off of the previous...and no matter what anyone says, there's always a second chance to make it better....or screw it up! ...I told myself I would keep up on the small amount of yard work I had this time so I wouldn't have to bust ass at a maniac pace to make it appear that I've kept up weeding, sweeping, trimming, few weeks before our landlord shows up...well, she had to come over to work on the patio and guess who nearly killed herself playing the "of course we take care of the outside of the house" game...and who was still caught short and had to pull all that damned Spanish moss mess that houses wolf spiders and fleas and other microscopic crap from the TREES holding a metal rake over her head....

    I just got a message from Windows Live Hotmail saying that they "check for spelling on the first 2000 characters. We're sorry, we couldn't check the rest of your mail." What the hell is that? You're a freaking computer. How about if I just decide, you know, I can only pay the first 2000 dollars for electric service. I'm sorry Progress Energy, but once we hit that lifetime total, I will be unable to pay the rest of your bills. Do they decide that after 2000 characters, no one has anything important to say, or that people just lose interest and stop reading? I'd say if a person has invested this much time into it, you should offer more services. Send that little guy out and start taking dictation.

    I do not envy your drive, especially with cats. Luckily, our dachshund travels well and is quite content to lie in one spot, eat Mickey D's French fries very politely from your hand, and pee on demand in rest stop parking areas. Be careful out there!!!!

Maureen

XXIV

The End of the Road

Sent: Friday, March 07, 2008 2:32 AM
Subject: The Rembis Report - Volume XXIV

On my way out of town one day, I passed the exit to Interstate 94 at it's Western terminus. You can't go any further west on that highway than Billings Montana. At that moment I had reflected upon its Eastern end - Port Huron Michigan. To be a bit more broad, I pondered mainly the area I-94 passes before it comes to a halt across from Canada: Detroit, Michigan.

I-94 cuts through the neighborhood I grew up in. A giant ditch of four lane concrete that separates Michigan Avenue from McGraw Street. It was here, standing at the Central Avenue bridge, we looked down and saw President Gerald Ford wave to us from the motorcade as they sped into downtown Detroit. Now, many years later, only days after considering what lies at both ends of this road, I was flying into DTW, Detroit Metropolitan Airport, and could see it below me coursing past farms and the giant Uniroyal tire that stands guard to welcome visitors to our famed Motor City - Detroit, the land of engines and optimism.

The flight from Billings to Minneapolis was crowded and beside me on all sides were chattering women. This is a sound I enjoy. I took no part in their conversations and vague interest in them as well, but their personable tones soothed me. More of the same from Minneapolis to Detroit. This time the ladies nearby shared with each other stories and even photos of their children and pets. Many men I know would have complained to no end about the high-pitched gossipy torrent, but not I. Hearing them delight in the camaraderie of motherhood was just what I needed to hear along with the drone of the jet engines on that particular day.

My hotel was quiet save for the guests who turned up their TV from 11:00 to midnight. No bother. Sleep did not want me, not until later anyway. In the morning, I visited my Mother before heading into the neighborhood. Like a car wreck, I did not want to see it as badly as I wanted to look. Before I got there I could only imagine what the house looked like after the fire that killed my sister.

When I lived in Tampa I volunteered at the Red Cross. I went on fire calls and awarded hotel, meal and clothing vouchers to those hapless victims who had lost everything. Fire is fast. And quiet. And devastating. What amazed me was the resilience of the people this happened to. They may have been in shock, but always seemed to be as calm as if their car had a dead battery and needed a jump. Never much to say, I guess because there was nothing to say. My Mom was the same way. She wasn't home at the time - she was at her chemotherapy appointment.

Imagine that. Your house burning down while you're at chemotherapy and losing your child.

Like other fire victims she was amazingly placid. She was grievous, of course, but her story is completely different from my

7751 Smart

Fathers'. He was there. This incident for him was much more fearsome than anything else he had ever experienced.

My Father has the same frame as myself, 5' 7", 200 pounds, 69 years old with an iron will. Third degree burns cover his head and hands. Sorrow pours from him.

9:00 AM. In the bathroom, the door shut. In the front room of the house, Marian slept on the couch or was watching TV. Beside her a candle burned. A cat roamed the house.

From inside the bathroom, he smelled smoke, then opened the door to an inferno. He reacted as any parent would and rushed to save his daughter.

Marian's willpower was much stronger than his. She froze in fear and did not move. Dealing with the fire for her, again, is a completely different story. 37 years old, 200 pounds, Marian had Downs Syndrome. She was so strong that he could not budge her. He tried. He described flames on her back and rushing to the sink to fill a pot of water to douse her. He pulled as hard as he could, her arms outstretched, he begged her to flee.

At her last conscious moment he knew it was too late and he saved himself. He could not have carried her.

The coroner ruled that smoke inhalation was indeed the cause of death.

The butterfly effect is one tiny move that starts a chain reaction. It's what causes us to sneeze when we don't know why. Perhaps a wisp of wind that started miles away drifted into the house that day and blew the curtain to the flame. It may have been the poor kitten my mother had adopted that tipped the candle. What deadly sprite sent a spark the wrong way? This we will never know.

Detroit and what happened to it has always held the same mystery for me. Detroit is a French phrase, *De Troit*, the straight. It describes how trappers viewed the Detroit River 300 years ago.

Proctor & Radcliffe

The history of Detroit is one of prosperity. We named cars, Cadillac, Pontiac after a French explorer, and a native Chippewa chief.

My Grandfathers came to Detroit in the 1930's and 40's to build these cars. It was a great place to raise a family. My parents met in the late 50's. In 1966 they bought a house across the street from the house my father was born in. That's where I grew up. I walked to school for twelve years and at some point it didn't feel safe anymore. The murder rate in Detroit was the highest in the nations history in 1977. The next four years through high school I walked quicker.

But what happened to Detroit? People still drive cars, now more than ever. I thought it was bad when I left in 1982, but look at it now.

I took these pictures the day of Marian's funeral. It wasn't this bad when I was a kid, but now they say it's the worst neighborhood in the city. In my opinion it is the worst neighborhood in the USA. My Mother's house is the brown one with the boarded windows. If you are from the neighborhood and haven't seen it in a while, you may recognize some houses, then again, maybe not. All of this is within a one mile radius. One thing I do know for sure, the store at Proctor and Radcliffe has been abandoned my entire life. How does this happen? The short answer is corruption according to many Detroiters. This article explores that question.

Broken rigs, broken hearts collide in deadly blaze
Detroit fire shows impact of budget cuts on safety
BY BILL McGRAW
The Detroit Free Press • February 27, 2008

After fire broke out in the front room of his home on Smart Street on Thursday morning, William Rembis fought the smoke and flames as he tried to save his daughter.

Chopin & Kirkwood

McDonald & Radcliffe

"I was choking and I had to get out," said the 69-year-old Rembis, his eyebrows singed, the burned skin on his hands, face and head raw and peeling. "I feel horrible about this."

But what he didn't know was that he also was battling the City of Detroit's budget problems -- problems that the fire union chief charges prevented the department from responding properly.

When the Detroit Fire Department dispatched rigs to the blaze, officials had to improvise. The department had taken two of the three closest pumpers out of service that day because they didn't have enough firefighters to staff them. The other one was closed permanently in 2005.

As a result, the first rig with all-important water on board had to travel from a longer than normal distance.

Marian Rembis, 37, died in the fire.

There is no way to determine if she would have lived had any of the three out-of-service pumpers been available, but the situation serves as a stark illustration of the way the city's money problems can impact public safety.

"This is the day we feared," said Dan McNamara, president of the Detroit Fire Fighters Association. "Our contention is they roll the dice every day in the city of Detroit. On this day, disaster struck."

In a statement, Fire Commissioner Tyrone Scott did not address specific questions in the Rembis home fire. He said several variables impact the response time of fire companies, including weather and traffic, and noted that the city has invested more than $28 million in the department over the past six years.

"A significant amount of the equipment is in disrepair because of factors that have nothing to do with the budget," Scott said, though he did not name them. "We also have to contend with constraining personnel issues that are mandated by provisions in the fire union contract, which greatly impact our ability to allocate resources."

Scott praised Detroit firefighters as "the best in the nation," and

McDonald Street

Dayton & McDonald

added: "The Detroit Fire Department mourns every single loss of life. It is a serious disservice to our community to presume that by singling out one factor for political purposes, you can determine the outcome in the event of a fire."

Widespread problem

Like all city departments, the Detroit Fire Department suffers from a lack of money, and officials have struggled with staffing and equipment problems for several years as the number of firefighters and rigs has been trimmed.

At times, the situation becomes acute, or someone dies, which focuses attention on the shortcomings -- which appear to be growing worse.

In May, the Free Press reported that 22% of the city's 66 firefighting vehicles either were unavailable to answer alarms or were working with broken equipment.

On the day Marian Rembis died, 27% of the fire vehicles were out of service or working with acknowledged defects -- such as ladder trucks with ladders that won't rise. Ten rigs in good condition sat idle in their quarters that day because the department couldn't staff them.

The problems play out every day, though mostly beyond public view.

Battalion chiefs, who supervise at fire scenes, sometimes can be heard on the radio begging dispatchers to send them a truck with a functioning ladder, even though their bosses discourage them from speaking so explicitly over public airwaves.

On Feb. 6, the first ladder truck -- Ladder 10 -- to arrive at the scene of what became a five-alarm fire at the Forest Arms apartment building near Wayne State University did not have a working ladder, but it was not needed to perform immediate rescues. Ladder

10's ladder has been broken since at least early January, firefighters said.

Holmes Street

5907 Elmer

In August, Scott, the fire commissioner, showed off 12 new rigs, costing $4.5 million. They replaced the 12 oldest vehicles in the fleet. But the city also is trying to cut the department further.

The union filed a lawsuit to block that plan. The case is now before the Michigan Supreme Court.

3rd rig fought the flames

The fire in the Rembis home, near Central and McGraw on the west side, started when a candle tipped over, William Rembis and arson investigators said. Marian, who had Down syndrome, was on a couch.

William Rembis was in a room in the back of the house when he realized what was happening. His wife, Julia, was at a hospital receiving chemotherapy treatment for cancer.

Rembis said his daughter panicked and refused to move. He filled a pan with water and tried to douse the burning couch. Eventually the flames and smoke forced him to flee.

Meanwhile, the first fire rig rolled up. It was Squad 4, a rescue unit that does not carry water or ladders.

Firefighters discovered flames bursting out of the home's façade and thought at first someone must have firebombed it. Rebuffed by the heat at the front porch, they raced to the rear and entered through the back door, but saw that flames and smoke had engulfed the room where Marian Rembis was sitting.

The second rig to arrive was Ladder 22, which is located nearby. It carries a small amount of water, but is not equipped to battle a roaring house fire, firefighters said. Engine 42, based at Livernois and I-96, arrived next. It was the first rig with the equipment to hook up to a hydrant and douse the fire.

The time sequence of the rig's arrivals was not available Tuesday.

Engine 42 is 2.24 miles from Smart and Central, according to MapQuest.

Holmes Street

Engine 34, the closest engine, which was out of service Thursday, is a mile away and would have had a more direct route to the blaze.

After the fire William and Julia Rembis buried their daughter Tuesday after a funeral mass at St. Cunegunda Church on St. Lawrence Street.

The church is near their home, which is now boarded up and decorated with a stuffed-animal memorial on the front steps.

William Rembis, who was born a few doors down from his charred home, talked about the fire this week and how he is haunted by his failure to get his daughter to safety, despite putting his own life at risk in the effort.

"I don't feel like a hero," he said, his eyes filling with tears. "I couldn't get her out."

He said each time he has walked down Smart Street since the fire, he imagines that the limbs of the trees are reaching out -- like his daughter reaching her arms out to him.

And that image haunts him.

"We took care of that girl all her life, and I couldn't save her."[10]

In addition to this newspaper article, on the internet archive, there are three pages of commentary and opinions by the locals. Some people directly blame Detroit's Mayor Kwame Kilpatrick for Marian's death.

It's not the Detroit I remember from the 1960's. I guess it started getting bad when I saw the National Guard roll down the street in tanks to quell the riots in 1967. Yes, I remember that. But I also remember days filled with happiness. Cars looked cool. It was safe to walk the street. A house fire was a rare thing.

Now in the neighborhood, when a child dies, stuffed animals are left in honor of the victim where they lived. By the day after the funeral it snowed and the few teddy bears that appeared the day before were joined by over a dozen more. Little consolation for any loss, but heartfelt condolence is greatly appreciated.

Marian used to carry around a piece of plastic. She must have just liked the texture in her hand. Not all the time, but a lot, she would hold a plastic Ziploc bag or a candy wrapper and just carry it around all day. In the pew at the church on the morning of the funeral, my parents sat together and a piece of plastic was mysteriously stuffed into the bench before them. A plain piece of nondescript clear plastic that Marian would have carried around with her. My Father mused it was her saying goodbye and that as she reached out in the fire, she wasn't reaching out to him, but to God.

How else would that piece of plastic have gotten there?

I didn't take pictures inside my Mother's house. The ceiling caved in where Marian died. Her brief visit with us ended tragically and if you think too much about it, you'll keep asking why and still never get an answer, and that can drive you nuts.

Like trying to figure out Detroit.

Detroit will never be the same, not in our lifetimes. But when the snow falls and blankets this scarred and dirty slum, you get a glimpse of what it once was. Before it was destroyed.

7715 Smart

XXV

A Change of Scene

Sent: Friday, April 04, 2008 10:08 AM
Subject: The Rembis Report - Volume XXV

Spidey was ready to leave. He had had enough. Cold. Snow. Tumbleweeds. He needed a change.

Not like Montana. Montana isn't going to change. Not any time soon anyway. Most states have several if not dozens of congressional representatives. Montana has only one, Denny Rehberg, who recently urged voters not to get swept up in Democratic calls for change, saying *"Change isn't always a good thing."*

As you know, politics are low on my agenda, but this sentiment echoes that of many central Montanans who are complacent with the way things are and always have been and that is why Mr. Rehberg will most likely be re-elected for a fifth term.

Not me. I need a change of scene every once in a while. I suppose that's why I travel as much as I do.

Einstein

Austin is proving to be a kaleidoscope of new tastes. There are over 7,000 restaurants here as well as endless entertainment venues. Plus, my opportunities to act have increased dramatically. 48 hours after my arrival I was on a movie audition and have two more auditions scheduled for next week. I also have appointments with two agents and expect to have solid representation very soon.

This is the second anniversary of The Rembis Report. When I began writing it I wondered as much then as I do now where I will be 25 issues later. At times, I know it may have read like an obituary column, so I'll take only a moment now to reflect on my dear little cat, Einstein, who recently passed after spending her 15 years on planet Earth with us. She is sorely missed.

I've been doing everything I can to promote BEST since the re-edit came complete. (Thanks again, Marcos!) I entered us into a few festivals and hopefully we will get noticed. The Banff World Television Festival would be a great place to be showcased because it focuses on TV shows. Since BEST is actually 33min 27sec it doesn't really fit into many festivals categories, but did qualify for the short film slots available at both the Port Townsend WA Film Festival and the Napa Sonoma Wine Country Film Festival so hopefully the festival coordinators will recognize our talent and add us to their rosters. There are no guarantees.

I do want to be taken seriously as a filmmaker and have been rejected by Sundance and other festivals of notoriety in the past, so I thought wouldn't it be a hoot to enter the Festival de Cannes, one of the most prestigious in the world. If you're going to have to face rejection in any way it might as well be from someplace reputable. They have a venue called the Short Film Corner for films under 35 minutes, so why not? The worst they could do is say "No, merci." So I entered. When I got the email confirming my entry and welcoming me to Cannes, I thought it was worded suspiciously, like I was in, that BEST would be showcased for all the world to see. They asked who I was bringing as a guest. My wife of course. I wouldn't mess that up. So I wrote back and asked if I was understanding everything correctly. Will BEST be shown at Festival de Cannes Short Film Corner? The answer: *"Oui. S'il vous plaît."*

The SFC is not a competition, but a market, with competitions within. All entrants will be showcased, including BEST. Since this is the case it would be best for me to go to Cannes to promote our work. According to the venue literature I need to get people into the viewing booths to punch in our number and watch the show. Who knows who will be there but most likely there will be a few executive producers trolling for fresh talent. BEST will also be digitized for viewing on the SFC website. And, what's really cool is that I am now authorized to place the Cannes 2008 SFC label on BEST to show I was there, kind of like a war medal.

So now the big trick is this - I need to get to France. Anybody got any frequent flier miles they don't need? Getting me to Cannes will ensure that you can all keep living vicariously through my quasi-self imposed image of success. I hitchhiked over 30,000 miles in the 1980's and I guess I'm now hitchhiking on a global scale.

Will I ever stop roaming? No, not according to my cell phone. A constant progression seems to be my fate. Every day begins a new journey and the end of the road is nowhere in sight.

Things are going to change. I think it's good.

XXVI

Life Goes On

Date: Thu, 1 May 2008 11:02 PM
Subject: The Rembis Report - Volume XXVI

The blank page beckons once more.
    I suppose I could sit here and stare at it until my forehead starts to bleed from the agony of trying to think of something to say - or I could say something.

Austin is proving to be a welcoming place. First the down side. There are beggars on many street corners. They await traffic with signs or sell candy with a "God Bless You" attached or wash windshields for beer money. It is as epidemic as gambling in Montana. There are no casinos here, so the addictions of the lost are fed by the charity of the masses and life goes on without missing a beat.

Now the up side. There are more opportunities for acting success here than anyplace else I have lived. I told you about the auditions I had last month - I was cast in a short film and will film the weekend after I return from Cannes. I've had several more auditions since then, have two more scheduled this weekend and I am now signed with Calliope Talent. Calliope is based in San Antonio and has a Los Angeles office so it may be feasible to actually audition for larger productions.

There is a strong talent networking group that meets here every month. I attended the meeting last night and introduced myself to the group, letting them know I'm looking for voice over work in addition to acting opportunities and was pleased to meet several studio executives and producers who exchanged contact information with me. Before I left Montana, I had the chance to cut a voice over demo the day I left for Texas. I placed a copy on my website. Listen if you wish, and share it with whoever you like, but please do not post my voice anywhere or I'll have to sue you and I don't want to do that.

It's amazing what gets out there on the Internet without your authorization. Surf around and you can see photos and video clips of celebrities used without their expressed written permission everywhere. In addition to the fan sites there are sites using content plagiarized from You Tube just to have something for some unknown reason. It happened to me. Why this page even exists is a mystery to be, but there is a site where you can watch five minutes of BEST and it's exactly what I have on my YouTube page.

Besides those sites officially sanctioned by me, the ones that I took some part in and added to my digital signature, there are other bizarre sites out there that use me and other actors for filler. This one didn't just grab my IMDb and YouTube stuff, it took BEST from Marcos Baca's YouTube page too! They also have a link for anyone wishing to submit nude pictures of me as well. Since no nude pictures of me exist, that I can recall, I am looking for a body double that we can use and just paste my head on. I am surfing as I write - there's another one! Again, I have no idea why. I also have a Chinese YouTube page and I have seen a Chinese IMDb page.

When you search for Mike Rembis on the Internet, don't be surprised if you run into one of these gentlemen - the other Mike Rembises:

Mike Rembis, Assistant Professor - History, University of Arizona

Mike Rembis, CEO, Centinela Freeman Hospital

Mike Rembis, Sun Microsystems, Ericsson Business Communications

All real high-tech guys. If I could get a hold of their resumes I'm sure I could get into some very interesting job interviews.

I could stand on a street corner and pass them out with my head shot.

XXVII

Cannes

Sent: Monday, June 02, 2008 8:20 AM
Subject: The Rembis Report - Volume XXVII

All of our problems would have been solved. Every financial woe relieved. The heart-shaped potato chip we pulled from the bag was going to transform our existence. Immediately, I told Ellen "Don't eat it! We can sell it on eBay!"

When we got home I gingerly carried it in on a napkin. Setting it on the counter in better light, however, it looked more like an ordinary potato chip than a heart-shaped potato chip. Not to be deterred, I searched eBay for comparable chips and lo and behold, there they were - THREE, count 'em - THREE different people selling heart-shaped potato chips, and much better looking than our alleged heart-shaped potato chip.

I had heard stories about potato chip collectors crazed to add to their collections, but this chip, even though I am no expert (of course French fries are another story) I could tell was nowhere near bizarre enough to warrant the fortune showered down by those eccentrics who would purchase a single potato chip only to place it on display. Our chip was pitiful by comparison, just as plain and ordinary as you could get with only a faint hint of a heartish cleave at the top, so I decided not to list it because I would hate to be embarrassed, scolded or shunned by the potato chip collecting community.

Can you imagine the public humiliation of trying to pass off a particularly shaped potato chip with this much competition when it is obviously below par? It's just not worth the risk.

I looked closer through the potato chip section and found a lips-shaped chip that the current owner is touting as similar in scale to Mick Jagger's or Angelina Jolie's.

With all this potato chip action going on I can only imagine people dumping out bags of chips to sort through them to find some elusive shape that is going to change the world as we know it. What will that chip be? The Microsoft Logo? A chip shaped like a German beer stein? Maybe a triangular potato chip that resembles a Dorito? These are questions that I am not likely to find the answers to because if there are already three other heart-shaped potato chips for sale right now, that means there are plenty of other people out there wasting time and effort for a starting bid of 99 cents and I wouldn't want to give these people more competition and drive their prices down further. That just wouldn't be right.

Besides that, I don't particularly want to be the guy that finds the world's strangest potato chip. I'd rather be known for doing something more creative, like making a movie about the guy who finds the world's strangest potato chip. But even that is something that's not on my roster. Not yet anyway.

I don't recall having any potato chips when I was in Cannes. I did have French Fries, which (I don't know why I thought this) I thought they would be called something different. But indeed, they call French Fries "French Fries" - even in France. They were good fries too. I should know. I am an expert. The other food I had wasn't just good - it was fantastic. The only reason for anybody to cook in France is because they are a chef. Each restaurant outdid or rivaled the next. Poultry and fish are succulent and tender. Chocolates and coffees are blended and brewed to perfection. Vegetables are crisp and breads are fresh, always. Even bartenders take extraordinary care in what they serve, crushing ice by hand, adding twists and garnish with militant precision. The culinary experience alone was worth the trip.

The main reason I went was to promote BEST at the Short Film Corner. To find my own little soapbox to stand on and tout my wares. There is no way to view every film at the SFC. There are thousands and it would take you weeks. The few that I did watch were remarkably well done, some obviously low budget, but the love of the craft shone through. I watched films from China, Lebanon, Belgium, the USA, and the UK. I was at the world premiere of WALTZ WITH BASHIR, a story of war set in 1980's Beirut and dramatized through animation and stunning special effects.

Walking the red carpet in Cannes is a spectacular experience. Cameras flash. Fireworks pop. Music blares triumphantly. The Grand Theatre Lumiere seats thousands and even halfway up in the balcony the seats are cushy and the view is perfect. It's the way all theaters should be.

There is so much energy in Cannes that you don't even know you've been up all night until you see that hint of light on the horizon. People from every aspect of film production are happy and willing to share a drink, small talk and even listen to your ideas. It truly is a place anyone in show business can go and find a fair playing field.

I was privileged in many ways on this trip. One session I

was accepted into was a "Pitch Training" class run by Ido Abram of the Maurits Binger Film Institute in The Netherlands. I don't know how many applicants there were but for the fifteen of us accepted I feel it was an invaluable experience. We all got to practice our style and learned to get our points across without haste or desperation. And it was fun.

I also entered the Cannes a la Flip Competition. I gave them a log-line and they gave me a little Flip video camera to shoot a three minute film with. I wrote a short called DOUBLE SUGAR and planned to find some actors and film it. The moment I got my camera, a man standing nearby told me about the Cannes 24 Hour Film Challenge and encouraged me to enter that too. I'm glad I did because I won.

I found three brilliant actors who were ready to make magic happen and we did. Following the 5 minute time limit and incorporating three product placements we made a little film called PERFECT PITCH. That was the title I drew along with the genre Buddy Comedy. It was noon on Sunday and I had 24 hours to finish my movie and place it on a USB drive. I finished it in a cyber-cafe down the street and was done by 11 PM. I went to turn it in and couldn't find anyone at the 24 Hours headquarters on the yacht. Where could they be? So I fretted most of the night, soberly protecting that tiny USB drive, getting home late and getting up early and I turned it in three hours prior to the deadline.

I must give a special thanks to all of the actors who helped me with these films. First, Pamela Holt, who starred in both of these films gave strong performances in both comedy and drama. For DOUBLE SUGAR she ran barefoot across the marina docks and unintentionally scuffed up her feet until they bled just to stay in character and keep continuity. That's true commitment and I can't thank her enough.

Judi Beecher was also tremendous as Pamela's friend in

our buddy comedy, PERFECT PITCH. Both of these ladies had such chemistry with Aymeric Hammad they simply brought in a truly fun performance. I personally had a hard time filming because I kept busting out laughing. Living in that moment watching their performance and filming it was one of the defining highlights of this trip and an absolute joy.

On my website you can watch DOUBLE SUGAR which also stars Ian Attfield, Matthew Jure and Angela Peters. Even though we were all pressed for time, these people helped me bring DOUBLE SUGAR to life in just a few hours.

Moments before we began filming we happened to be sitting near composer Ruth Chan who offered me a CD with a few different cuts of music that were available for use. I am so glad. She had a perfect piece that serves as the background for this little thriller. Finally, thanks to Rebecca Jameson, who has a two second cameo in the last scene and acted as my personal assistant throughout the entire shoot, helping scout locations and carrying my bag.

Thank you all again so much. Hopefully, IMDb will recognize me as a director/producer with talents like these in my films. Time will tell.

I have a lot of editing to do. I plan to take some of the footage from these shoots and create new shorts without the 3 and 5 minute time restraints and enter new versions into other festivals. I also have screenplays to edit and I need new head shots too. I did take a few minutes to edit the home video I took of the trip and because what happens in Cannes goes on the internet if you click to my YouTube page you can see my entire week whittled down to under nine minutes. It includes footage of my adventures, the Cannes red carpet and the guy who accidentally locked himself in the men's room stall at the disco.

As soon as I got home I was right back in front of the camera again. I acted in a short film last week entitled LATE. Drew

Ott, a young gentleman with subtle demeanor, directed us and took great care in setting up his shots. His short film is part of an online film festival called the Time Fest.

I also have an audition for another film scheduled a few weeks from now.

But I'm not the only one getting cast. If you have time check out one of my BESTest friends Vicki Wayne in the POSH (Players Of Safety Harbor) stage production of The Supporting Cast. And if you have even more time take a closer look inside your next bag of potato chips. Elvis Presley might be in there.

From the Response File
Volume XXVII

Received: Thursday, June 12, 2008 12:18 PM
Hi Mike,
How are things?!!! all sounds FAB there with you!!!

Firstly, HUGE CONGRATS on your big PRIZE!!! That's fantastic!!! You're a STAR!!!!!!!!

Secondly, A HUGE SORRY - my many, many apologies for my lack of contact / replies. Have had massive sagas recently and have been 100% out of the loop.

Thirdly, a HUGE, HUGE, HUGE for the credits on 'Double Sugar'. I am so proud to have the award winning Mike Rembis on my CV!!! It was so FAB to meet you - what an inspiration - you just DID IT!!!!!! thanks for your lovely comments in your email - you are FAB! I can't wait to catch up next Cannes - will probably do what you did and go for an earlier part next time. But let's def keep in touch - i love your email updates on what you are doing - what a fab idea!

I am slowly getting through all my emails now - so sorry for the delay Mike - my apologies.

You take care and a huge congrats from me on everything you are doing :)))))

and p.s. will def be there some point the weekend for the Marbella

FF - I saw mac there at same place at another thing on tues and he told me about it - thanks for the tip shall look out for Barbara.
    Thanks for passing it on - that's so lovely of you.
    Rebecca Jameson

XXVIII

Generosity

Sent: Wednesday, July 02, 2008 9:34 PM
Subject: The Rembis Report - Volume XXVIII

Generosity is mysterious.
    I had a much more eloquent sentence to explain that, but once again, I pushed the wrong button and my exacting prose was erased and my thoughts left scrambled.
    When I hitchhiked so many miles to and fro across the country in the 1980's I never wondered why people gave me rides. I put out my thumb and I got where I was going. I had a purpose. A reason to go from here to there. Those who gave me the rides to reach "there" however, had no reason to stop other than they were going that way, so they did. I had long rides - the longest from Limon, Colorado to Dunkirk, New York, and rides as short as a block. My drivers did not want anything. I was fortunate enough to meet many more good people than bad. Some friends I met while hitchhiking I still keep

in contact with and are recipients of this newsletter. One of them asked me "Do you pick up hitchhikers?"

"No." I answered "Most times I don't."

I rarely see them. When I do, I find myself with work piled on the front seat or going too fast to stop in time, or sometimes, they just look dirty. I can't remember exactly, the last time I gave somebody a ride, but I know it was in Montana on Interstate 90. A short and uneventful encounter.

Here in Texas, I see a lot of panhandlers, people on street corners, not with upraised thumb seeking a destination, but with outstretched cup asking for a cash donation. I never give them anything. It seems as epidemic here as casinos are in Montana. At some intersections you may find as many as four or five beggars.

Yesterday, I saw one man lower his cardboard sign to chat with another man hauling a backpack. They stood on the median beside I-35 and shook hands and appeared to speak cheerfully. The man with the backpack had his own cardboard sign tucked under his arm. They stood toe to toe as jovial colleagues, like attorneys or businessmen on Wall Street, recounting the latest news or the day's events. They waved farewell and the man with the backpack ambled on. The other man resumed his business at hand and displayed his sign to the vehicles trapped at the red light. It read something like "Please help, God bless."

How profitable is this? Who supports these people? And the most curious question of all - Why?

For the last few months I have slowly woven myself into the fabric of the Austin acting scene. I meet with actors networking groups. I joined the Texas Film and Television Alliance. I helped found a small production group.

We recently chose a short screenplay to produce. I am the casting director. At our meeting the other night, two new members volunteered their services to seek donations for the group. Donations?

We're a for-profit group! Why would anybody donate anything to us? I could not fathom such a concept. Each of the other members of the group agreed wholeheartedly with the concept of asking restaurants and stores for donations to feed the cast and crew. I alone was dumbfounded. Again - Why? What's the motive? What's in it for them? Actors and crew looking to build their resumes, locations I could understand, even props to borrow and return, I've asked for those, but free food? "Who is going to do that?" I asked.

"You'd be surprised." they told me.

Austin apparently has a huge heart. This is the general consensus among the group. Ask and ye shall receive. Keep Austin Weird. These folks are completely positive that we will get everything we need to make our little film absolutely free.

I just can't wrap my mind around it. You want something, you buy it. Maybe there's some haggling over price, some negotiation, but free just doesn't fit into the equation. For as mathematically challenged as I am even I know that 0 = 0 not SOMETHING = 0. That's like breaking the laws of physics. Like traveling back in time or going faster than light - it's just not going to happen.

But it is happening. I can't explain how or why, but it is, and all I can do is marvel at it. The panhandlers are living proof. As predictable as sunrise, they will be out there - you can count on it. The intersection at US Highway 183 and Cameron Road is commanded by four men who sell half liter bottles of water. I don't know what they charge. This is common. You could hardly consider them panhandlers because they are engaged in supply and demand commerce. On other corners I have seen those at first glance to be panhandlers selling toys or candy. There are very few that are old school enough to squeegee your windshield, and unfortunately, they don't have any water buckets, but they are out there, too. And the only reason they are is because of the seemingly constant generosity bestowed by the drivers.

Even if I had never gotten a ride when I hitchhiked I don't know that I would have stopped. It is as much an addiction as pumping coins into a machine that does nothing. So I can practically guarantee that panhandlers will maintain their stance on these corners whether they are placated or not.

I find this to be an odd and curious aspect of society, even as I find myself to be a beneficiary of it. How do the givers prosper? Magnanimous philanthropists who give billions of dollars to charity, of course, realize that they are doing something for the greater good, to secure some facet of humanity. They may even enjoy some tax break as a result, feel good in the process and truly lose nothing because they have so much it can never all disintegrate. Hotel magnate and billionaire Leona Helmsley left her fortune to care for her puppies.

But what of those who putter along and fill their tanks at the station for a penny less than the place across the street? Do they give those pennies to the men and women standing by the side of the road? Some do. No tax break. No question of "Should I?" Just a simple gift tossed out the window to a stranger.

I had a photo session yesterday. The photographer took about 200 pictures of me for new headshots. Our conversation naturally led to our daily lives and how we fill our time when not fulfilling our dreams of being behind or in front of a camera. She volunteers. She and her friends rebuild trails in municipal parks around Austin. They are paid a pittance, but they do it for the love of the outdoors, not for the paycheck. Her assistant who held the light board to bounce shadows away from me was also one of those volunteers. I am finding that this is the typical Austinite. They do what they love. People standing at the intersections with signs do not particularly disturb them, and if they do, they haven't said so.

How strange this world of ours.

I sold cars years ago. Charlie was a crusty old salesman who had fumbled around the lot for the last forty-odd years, as much a fixture as the neon sign above us. He always had customers. Generations of people sought out his advice and trusted him. I wondered about the sheer number of new cars along the avenue, not just at our lot, but all of them and asked him "How can there be this many cars for sale? Who's going to buy them all?"

Charlie told me "There's an ass for every seat."

So it must be with the symbiotic nature of charity. Somebody must feel the need to give as much, and perhaps more, than those in need.

Thank goodness. What would the world be without those who believe that it is better to give than to receive? How would we ever get anywhere?

Soon, I am going to ask a favor of all of you. I will have my new headshots in a few days and I will need to choose one to represent me. I know from past experience that it is unwise to choose your own headshot. Nobody really looks the way they think they do. I decided to use my own abs instead of hiring a body double so as a result there will be no photos depicting my abs. When I get the photos, I will email you a link and if you would be so kind as to take a look and pick one that looks like me after you stop laughing, this gesture would be greatly appreciated. I just need to know - which Mike Rembis would you cast?

I have been acting.

Last week I played a U.S. Border Patrol Agent in THE FALLING MAN and I was an extra in two scenes for DEEPER AND DEEPER starring Emmy Winner David Lago. I also have an upcoming role in a feature called THE WHY.

You can also catch me in the recently completed dark comedy, LATE.

Thank you for reading The Rembis Report. Your kindness knows no bounds.

THE HEAD SHOTS

I sent about three dozen photos out to the Rembis Report recipients along with this short note.

Sent: On or about on Friday, July 18, 2008

Yes, this is it. These are the infamous recent head shots I warned you about.

If you would be so kind as to take a look at each one, and when you finish laughing, choose the ones that look the most like a professional serious actor, please email me with your choices. Each one is labeled with 4 digits. The ones that get the most votes are the ones I will use for my website and other marketing. The ones that get the least votes may be pinned to your dartboard.

I look forward to your responses and will let you know the outcome of the popular vote in the next Rembis Report.

Thanks,
Mike Rembis

Received: Saturday, July 19, 2008 12:04 AM

I like the first one, #9255, you seem the most natural and have sincere eyes. Of course I do want to reach in and button your shirt one more button, but that's just me.

Sincere eyes. It's a compliment. Unfortunately, it does sound like a disease, "what happened to him? oh, poor guy. Got sincere eye. Too bad, he was so young."

Have a great weekend. It's raining so much down here and so hot outside at the same time it's like trying to breathe through one nostril with your head covered in a plastic bag. Gotta love Florida summers.

Maureen

Received: Saturday, July 19, 2008 2:25 AM
Hello Mike

The two photos that I have chosen for you are those that I consider the most natural. Does that count in acting? Go get em.

Richard.

P.S. - The suit looks a bit large for you, been dieting to lose all that weight you gained in Cannes?

The Runner Up

XXIX

My Last Sale

Sent: Sunday, August 03, 2008 3:59 PM
Subject: The Rembis Report - Volume XXIX

It's almost midnight and it's 97 degrees F in Austin. We are at the edge of a record-breaking heatwave here. It may, and probably will become, the hottest summer on record. It's the kind of weather that keeps you inside to revel in the luxury of air conditioning. Days like this even make you wonder why you left Montana. But it gets hot there too. Then I look at my blossoming acting resume and remember that there is no acting work up there.

I have a friend who post-scripts all of his messages with this note: *Keeping busy keeps you busy*. I find now that after separation from my nine year role as an advertising salesman I am busier than ever. In my application for a writing fellowship, in addition to 500 words or less on why I want to write for television, it was required that I also include my autobiography. In four pages I found the story of my life to be quite worthwhile. I am certain the review panel will remain entertained and that my spec script for an episode of Boston Legal will be well received. In recounting my tale that spans the last 30 years or so, most of the work I have done came down to an acting job. I went to acting school, in part, so that I could memorize my sales pitch. A year later I was deemed Sales Professional of the Year for the Florida West Coast Division. I got my name on a plaque and applause from my co-workers and the whole time, I never saw it coming. I was just acting the part of a salesman.

I've acted the role of a salesman many times. Cars and trucks, appointments for services, retail items. Twenty years ago, I worked a short time in Van's IGA in Bozeman, making take-and-bake pizzas. A man I recognized bought a cheese pizza, thanked me, and left. It bothered me an hour later when I knew I recognized him but couldn't remember from where. I looked in the cash register at the check he wrote for seven dollars. It was a local bank. The Flying D Ranch business account. Ted Turner signed it. It still took a moment to click that I had just sold a pizza to a billionaire. My biggest client, my smallest sale, ever.

It was a nice, quiet, low-key environment. It was so simple, I didn't need to put a lot of effort into that act. Not like I did down the street at Pizza Hut, where the manager was thrilled to be there and you should be too. I told my boss there I considered my role at the time more of a social experiment than a career. (I still didn't know I was an actor). He didn't like that. I was studying psychology at the time and was just being honest with him. Most employers don't care for honesty. I delivered for Dominos for a week or two in Moses Lake Washington. Since they had a company car, I used that. When it broke down, I refused to use my own and had to make pizzas while the manager made deliveries with his car. A customer asked me "What's the best thing about working here?"

I told the truth, "Walking out that door."

I was soon ordered not to talk to customers.

So now, in addition to seeking acting work as an actor, I am also seeking a new act, the kind where you sign a W-2 and get some pittance for doing something nobody else will do. Not having been on a job search for nearly a decade, and for all intents and purposes, the first time in this millennium, I'm finding that having a solid 40-hour-a-week work ethic combined with a relaxed attitude about results was lost somewhere around 1994. The glory days of saying "I can breathe and see and probably won't embarrass you, so you should hire me" are gone. People don't just want to hear you've had a job before and showed up on time, they want to hear numbers. How many sales you had, where you ranked among peers at local, regional, and national levels, how many calls you made on a daily basis, what your quotas and goals were. Who keeps track of all that? I'll tell you who - people that don't act for a living, that's who.

It's tough out here for a working actor. All I'm looking for is a script and a call time. How you edit the results is your business.

A lot of jobs, and apparently the majority, expect you to plan your entire future around their agenda. I keep finding companies that are seeking not just team members, but lifetime partners. They boast the command of their enterprise having the greatest employees who love to be there and superiority to their competition who fear them. The common theme is simply this - *There is no better place to work.*

That level of pride is what astonishes me the most. Companies and the behaviorally produced management put into place fiercely defend this theme and are building nearly impenetrable walls to keep actors out. Thus, they maintain a majority of employees who blanket the walls of these fortresses with trust that the company will protect them because they are a valuable and irreplaceable asset.

In most cases, this is not true. When you look at a gigantic corporation, there is no cog that can not be replaced. No job is safe. After nine years, even though I acted the role superbly, asking for the transfer to Austin, I was denied. It had nothing to do with performance or tenure. It was simply a matter of head count. At the Mad Hatter's table, there was no more room.

So, high on a dusty hill north of Billings, my final bow came with a sale to a man who ran a kennel. He shook my hand and thanked me for the good deal on his advertising and the nice art work I had created. For him, it was not an act. He loves to see the dogs come in and out and let them run together when the pet owners allow it.

All the world is a stage and so many people don't even know it. They are not acting. They believe in what they do and display true emotions. Were it not for people who show us their actual selves, speak their thoughts and live their convictions, actors would have no one to portray. Thanks to real people we find something to do that keeps us busy. And as long as actors remain in the workforce doing what they must to survive, real people will be faced with live performance forever, and never know if who they are dealing with are genuine or not.

In the real world of acting, my good friend Matthew Jure, who was the man strangled in the opening sequence of my film DOUBLE SUGAR, has jumped the pond to star as Sexy Rexy in STARLIGHT AND SUPERFISH, now being filmed in Detroit! You look fantastic Matthew. I hope that's not a wig and you let your hair grow and bleached it blond like I suggested.

I acted in a short retelling of Edgar Allen Poe's THE TELL TALE HEART as a police detective and had a couple great monologues in a feature called THE WHY. I'll keep you posted on what happens with those. Thank you all for participating in choosing my headshot. The overwhelming majority voted for 9255 as the winner.

I thought the shoot was okay, but got a boo and a hiss from my agent. Valerie Tamburri, the photographer, didn't like that and graciously got right to work on a second shoot for me. Two hundred frames later we found one that my agent should give a thumbs up.

Part of the hard work I'm doing these days includes casting for the short film PEOPLE THAT DO SOMETHING which we plan to shoot in two weeks and then I should be flying out to Los Angeles to co-direct another short film called SETTLE. I'll keep you updated on those projects too.

Don't forget to keep me updated on what you're up to so I can tell everybody else what's up.

In the meantime, I plan to keep busy, keep acting and stay cool.

You do the same.

The Chosen One

XXX

Politicalism

Sent: Monday, September 1, 2008 11:39 PM
Subject: The Rembis Report - Volume XXX

Okay, don't get all excited. It means 30, NOT *intended for mature audiences only*. Yes, we have hit the two and a half year mark with The Rembis Report. I am sure you are as amazed as me. As long as you keep reading, I'll keep writing.

Hurricane season is in full force. Not only the real ones battering the gulf coast and inching toward the Eastern seaboard, but the figurative political ones as well. So many people deemed as conservative traditionalists who would never vote for a woman or a black man now find that to maintain that position would result in balloting some lesser known independent party or casting no vote at all. Decisions. Decisions. To evolve or not to evolve? That is the question.

You know that I rarely wax politics into my musings, however, as of this writing, I am at the keyboard of my late father-in-laws computer. This must have something to do with it because he always encouraged Ellen and I to get more heavily involved in the bloodlines of government. I suppose I may be channeling his essence in some way, parked beneath one of his odd paintings, filled with random phrases, opinions, and prose that reek of free speech and makes some statement about the constitution and government that is only decipherable by one's own interpretation.

Looking at this painting and trying to explain it to you is like offering my viewpoint of an amendment I do not fully understand. Since a picture says a thousand words, I'll let it do the talking and see if you can figure it out for yourself.

If you think this is confusing, have you ever thought about the difference between a Republican and a Democrat? According to Webster's Revised Unabridged Dictionary the definition of a Republican

is: One who favors or prefers a republican form of government. And the definition of a Democrat is: One who is an adherent or advocate of democracy, or government by the people.

Okay, I think at this point I should explain that the high school I went to was a public entity that passed a lot of people who couldn't read, so I'm not sure how to interpret either of those definitions. If I'm right, this means that Republicans don't advocate the Democratic process and that Democrats don't want a Republican form of government which loops us back to the original question - what's the difference? Don't we live in a Republic with a Democratic process? And if we do, what exactly does that mean?

Rather than confuse you any further with Catch-22 examples I can't explain anyway, I'd rather steer you toward some websites that can't explain it either, but have tried.

One website, which is run by conspiracy theorists who plainly say there is no difference, post this message: "THIS DEMOCRAT PARTY VS REPUBLICAN PARTY ARTICLE IS NOT COPYRIGHTED.

Exhibit 30A
Original Painting by Raymond Wittek

YOU ARE FREE AND ENCOURAGED TO PASS THIS CRITICAL INFORMATION ON TO AS MANY FELLOW AMERICANS AS POSSIBLE. POST IT AND EMAIL IT NOW TO AT LEAST 10 PEOPLE!" Apparently my own curiosity has made this happen.

Another site is run by yet another conspiracy theorist who considers him/herself to be 88% Republican. After a full page of explaining the differences between the two we learn this individual's true agenda: *"The war on drugs is ripping this country apart. This is where a 7/8th-nation is born. I disagree with the Republican party's aspect on the war on drugs. There is only one solution to this; control, regulation, and extreme financial gain. This would almost overnight eliminates the United States Federal funds burden."*

This one http://home.earthlink.net/~votersguide/vs.html gives some clearly defined pros and cons and leans toward being Republican. If you'd like to get a slightly more Democratic point of view check out this series of parodies of the Mac/PC ads http://www.youtube.com/view_play_list?p=EDA39C7414910E68

If you'd like to get really confused log into Madam Lichtenstein's Cosmic World http://thestarryeye.typepad.com/newage/2008/03/democrats-vs-re.html to see her astrological prediction that says it's going to be close between the two parties this year. Who'd-a thunk it!

Finally, if you really need to know what's going on with the candidates this year and can't decide between the Democrats or Republicans, you can find out who else is running for President on Wikipedia. http://en.wikipedia.org/wiki/2008_Presidential_Candidates This spreadsheet will introduce you to all of the candidates and explain who could actually get a majority vote if they had an extra 20 - 40 million dollars to pay for advertising and let people know they exist.

If you're stuck on the old strategy of the Archie Bunker archetype and feel the need to vote for two white guys, Chuck Baldwin, Bob Barr, Ralph Nader, and their running mates welcome your vote.

Or, you can get the best of both worlds and push the button to elect Green Party candidate Cynthia McKinney. When you think about it, she's all the candidates rolled up into one - a black woman with an Irish name whose running mate is independent journalist and Hip-Hop activist Rosa Alicia Clement. You can't get more down home *Repudemoculan than that.

On the acting front, I had the unique privilege to be a background extra on a few scenes in FRIDAY NIGHT LIGHTS, which films in Austin. This is FNL's third season and I was in two scenes with their latest starring cast member, the lovely Janine Turner, BKA Maggie O'Connell from Northern Exposure and that lady from Cliffhanger with Sylvester Stallone.

I got to sit in the stadium a section away from Ms. Turner, managed to snap a few photos and also worked a restaurant scene where I was given one of the best props I ever had to work with. A plate of lamb chops.

This month we also got a nice little short film in the can, PEOPLE THAT DO SOMETHING, written by Marlayna Glynn Brown and Directed by Aiah Samba. I am an Executive Producer and acted as casting director and location manager. Here's a shot of our cast on set. Back: Ben May, Jane Butler. Front: Gary Wimmer, Kathryn Olsen. It's a great little story about a fellow who takes his step-daughter shoplifting. Editing is under way and I'll keep you updated on when and where to catch it. Thanks to everyone involved in doing a fantastic job.

For those who find themselves in London this month, please try and catch my friend Matthew Jure in the stage comedy PAINTING BY NUMBERS playing at The Old Red Lion Theater. The show opens tonight and runs until September 20.

Exhibit 30B
Janine Turner

Exhibit 30C
Friday Night Lights

Exhibit 30D
Cast of People That Do Something - Back: Ben May, Jane Butler - Front: Gary Wimmer, Kathryn Olsen

Exhibit 30E
Lamb Chops - Before

Exhibit 30F
Lamb Chops - After

And keep me updated on what you're doing too, so I can pass it along to everybody else out there. The Rembis Report now reaches over 200 people every month and I'm sure it's just going to get worse as time goes on.

Enjoy the late days of summer and try to stay out of the rain - unless you can't.

*Repudemoculan [re-pew-de-mah-kew-lahn]

-adjective

1. Of or pertaining to repudemoculan ideas.

-noun

1. A person who sees no true distinction and can not tell the difference between a Democrat and a Republican. e.g., Mike Rembis.
2. George W. Bush's favorite word.

(The ideas expressed in this newsletter are formulated as the result of a public education and over 25 years in the US workforce compounded by lots of TV. Those taking offense are advised to get a sense of humor. At Wal-Mart.)

XXXI

Austin

Sent: Wednesday, October 1, 2008 11:27 PM
Subject: The Rembis Report - Volume XXXI

The house looked just fine before we bought it. As usual.
It didn't need any work. Nothing at all. Not one single thing was broken. But over the months we have lived here somehow a new refrigerator showed up. Then a new stove, I think, maybe not in that particular order, but a new dishwasher showed up too, one day. And a new sink basin. I seem to recall this being the case in my last three houses, too. It all looked good the day we moved in. Everything worked. We were golden.

But then, something just wasn't right. Sometimes a smell showed up. A faint dismissible odor by most accounts that when you stood in the kitchen too long, no longer remained something to be ignored. Even after cleaning the refrigerator, or tightening the gas lines, those older appliances had seen better days and we retired them to welcome new appliances that wished they had found better homes and gardens, but wound up at our house instead.

New washing machines have cropped up too. Sometimes when I'm alone in a parking lot, or at the grocery store, or in a gas station, I feel as if I am being stalked by an appliance salesman. They see me nearby and they know; "That guys going to need something major. He's buying the small ice cream. That means his freezer's going out."

We have remodeled every one of our homes. Sometimes a little, sometimes a lot. We replaced a fence at one house and now it looks like we are about to do it again. Yes, it's an old fence, wooden and crumbling. It's 13 years old and ready to fall should a violent wind whip through the yard. Yet, it didn't look like a fence we would be replacing so soon the day we moved in. How did that fence look so good six months ago? It's falling down around us - it's hideous! An atrocity! What evil hypnotic forces are at work here? How did we not see this?

I don't know. But I do know that replacing this particular item is going to be an adventure because never before have we had to deal with (drum roll, please) the Home Owners Association.

When I mentioned this to the fence man giving the estimate, he looked like he had just met Fred Munster. "You don't want to deal with them if you don't have to. They can take your house away if you make the wrong improvements and try to fight them. They are the epitome of evil. It's not good if you don't do what they say." He shook his head and looked down at the ground knowing that there may be no true way to get his proposal past the residential committee. He slumped back to his truck envisioning his request to work on our house being pored over by them, the deciders, (cue sad music) and the insane laughter of the association chairman.

Imagine, wanting to work on your own home and do what you want with it and not being able to. It can happen. We already know we'll end up taking the cheap way out and replacing this fence with the same boring wooden style just to make it easy, but I'm seriously considering submitting a bunch of proposals that absolutely won't fly in this neighborhood just to waste their time, for no other reason than because I can. You see, you can't start work on your fence without approval, so the longer it gets held up in their file of inadequacy (cue laughter), the longer it will take them to inspect what's really going on here. That will give me ample time and opportunity to take the really cheap and easy way out - replacing one board at a time.

They would never notice. We have approximately 534 slats that surround our yard and already had one fall out that I replaced in a matter of minutes. If I did, say, 20 boards every weekend, I could have a new fence in 6 months using the existing posts and not have to hire anybody. Kind of a "pay as you go" home improvement method. If the Home Owners Association ever did point out that some of our fence was old and some new, we could simply tell them "Those were the boards we had to replace. You still haven't approved our plans for the chain link or the plastic. What's taking you so long?" They would never approve chain link or plastic in this community. The fence guy assured me of that.

So we'll see. Right now, it's just an idea. But so was the notion that we were moving into a place that didn't need any work.

Think that's ridiculous? Get this - I had another gig on Friday Night Lights tonight and got to watch them throw a football around. They gave me a great meal, lots of snacks, never pointed the camera at me, then wrapped and sent me home three hours after I showed up on set. They still paid me for eight hours so it's not really so bad. A tank of gas for standing around and communing with fellow actors for a little while is worth it.

But I did some real acting this week, on a show slated for web cast: STRIPPERS HAVE MORE FUN THAN ANYBODY. It's a fun little comedy coming soon to a computer near you. I play Alek

Christopoulous, the owner of the Pink Monkey, where Evangeline decides to get a job just to make a bit of quick cash to get caught up on bills. But somehow, Evangeline quickly gets caught up in all the fun that strippers have and can't seem to quit. I'll let you know when it's on line. Don't get too excited. There's no nudity. It's a stripper comedy for the whole family.

My producers group, The Austin Filmmakers, now has 100 members, but really, only about 5 - 7 of us ever show up for the meetings. But that doesn't mean we're not doing anything. PEOPLE THAT DO SOMETHING is almost out of the editing bay and we started casting for two more short comedies.

I have been keeping busy with my writing, tweaking portions of scripts in progress, and recently completing a short script I am really proud of because I was hired to write it. UNPUNISHED is a page from the sad history of the Femicides of Ciudad Juarez, Mexico. Since 1992 hundreds of women have gone missing in Northern Mexico and their bodies, if they were found at all, have been abused and butchered. No criminals have ever been brought to justice and there is strong evidence of police involvement and corruption to hide that involvement in these murders. Jennifer Lopez made a movie about this a few years ago. BORDERTOWN explores the subject from the perspective of a reporter and a survivor of abduction and torture. Unpunished takes the viewpoint of a missing girls' family and the sister determined to find her. Our project has been endorsed by Amnesty International and goes into production next month. The Director, Din S. Altit, hopes you will support the effort to give these women a stronger voice since they can no longer shout for themselves.

The more writing I do, the more I find I need just one more creative outlet once in a while. Editing is something that I am starting to enjoy. Sometimes I'm not so great about saving files the right way, but I do get a few things accomplished. When I saw the chance to win a trip for two to the Cannes Film Festival next year, I jumped on it. I dusted off the tapes from our trip to the Gobi Desert and put together a one minute film called THE MONGOLIAN DEATH WORM for the Short Circuit / Dailymotion competition. This work was my first film and originally 20 minutes long, but since the rules said they needed 60 seconds or less, I took what I felt was the essence of it and uploaded it to my Dailymotion page.

If you've got more than a minute to have a laugh, check out STATEN ISLAND SOPRANO on my YouTube page, my homage to the opening credits of The Sopranos featuring my dear, sweet wife, Ellen.

My editing may not be the best, but it's fun. Speaking of BEST, I figured out how to rip files from a DVD and re-edit them, so I cut a ten minute version of BEST, but the file isn't compatible with anything else but DVD technology, so I can't upload it to the web, not even my own website. Oh well, at least I'll be able to show it this Tuesday night, when I'll be the headlining guest on The Infynit Hour on Austin's Cable Channel 10. It's not simulcast on the web, so if you'd like to catch it, get to Austin quick!

Finally, congratulations to Drew Ott, who will be joining the Austin Film Festivals Young Filmmakers competition this year with LATE, a film he had the genius to cast me in. Drew runs a professional set and his hard work has paid off. I myself entered a short film and a screenplay into the major categories this year and didn't get in. I did however, thanks to Ellen, find myself signed on with a Producers Pass and two pitch competition tickets. I'm brushing up on those pitches every day.

The festival starts in two weeks. I understand there's a convoy of semi tractor trailers hauling hard liquor on its way here that's slowing down interstate traffic.

I think it's going to be fun.

XXXII

When Larry Met Mikey

Sent: Sunday, November 2, 2008 2:33 AM
Subject: The Rembis Report - Volume XXXII

In keeping this diary, trying to post something on the first day of every month, I find I reflect more on each Halloween because it falls on the last day of the month. For those faithful readers of The Rembis Report, you know that the last two were a bust. Almost no trick or treaters in Montana. Not so in Austin. It was great. The little monsters came in droves and we ran out of candy. I put my camera up in the tree and videotaped myself scaring children, but since nobody got exceptionally scared and ran into a wall or anything, I didn't get any spectacular footage. I put on the werewolf mask and growled when I answered the door. Some kids laughed. One little Darth Vader didn't even flinch. The light saber looked real. He got two pieces of candy. Then I pulled the old headless man gag and dropped candy indiscriminately, mostly missing their sacks and hitting the walkway and the children laughed and scrambled for it, so a fun time was had by all.

I attended the Austin Film Festival this month. A multitude of writers have descended here for the last 15 years and those most successful hold panels and conferences to share wit and wisdom. I met several writers and directors whose names you may not know, but whose work you have probably seen. I walked Greg Daniels across the street from the panel he was finishing to his next engagement that I had planned to attend. Since he found himself being escorted by me, he supposed that I was somehow involved with the administration and he introduced me to his parents and brother, who came to watch him receive an award for Outstanding Achievement in TV Writing. Although I couldn't tell him more about BEST, due to conflicts (he is not allowed to listen to pitches), we did have a lively conversation and he gave me some valuable insight on the inner workings of FOX and NBC. Greg Daniels was Conan O'Brien's roommate and fellow writer on both Saturday Night Live and The Simpson's before he helped Mike Judge (who wrote Beavis and Butthead) develop King Of The Hill. He now leads the writing team for The Office. I also met Dan Petrie, Jr. who was thrilled to sign my autograph book because nobody ever asks him for his autograph. He wrote Beverly Hills Cop. I also got to meet actors Tom Skerritt (Alien, M*A*S*H, Picket Fences), James Cromwell (W, The Queen, 24) and movie director Danny Boyle (28 Days Later, Trainspotting, A Life Less Ordinary). Tom Skerritt was in a hurry to go somewhere and didn't spend much time talking to fans. James Cromwell accidentally broke my Sharpie, but he put it back together. We had just watched the world premiere of W, where he plays George H.W. Bush. Danny Boyle was thrilled to accept his award for Outstanding Achievement in Filmmaking and was there for his World Premiere of Slumdog Millionaire.

One of the most fascinating panels I visited was a conversation with Lawrence Kasdan. He wrote Raiders Of The Lost Ark, The Empire Strikes Back, Return Of The Jedi, Grand Canyon, The Big Chill, and Silverado, just to name a few. I had the chance to ask him a question so I did. The one lingering question that I had wondered about for years since I first saw the movie in 1981, now I had the writer of the movie right there in front of me so I asked "What is the purpose of the clown in Body Heat?"

You may recall a clown driving a car that really seems to have nothing to do with the story, but it's there and you can't forget it. I have gone over the scene in my mind dozens of times and had multiple conversations on this very subject and have never heard what I considered to be a satisfactory answer. So here I was, ten feet away from the man who wrote and directed the very movie, and when I asked him the question that had dug into my skull for 27 YEARS with no good answer he said to me "That's a very good question. Many people have asked that."

He said it in a sarcastic sort of way, which of course I can't help but admire, the group chuckled and then he pointed at somebody else and said "Next question."

The one thing that Lawrence Kasdan did say, the golden nugget of knowledge most writers shared, is that you have to write your stories for yourself, not for anyone else. Even if you find yourself hired to write something for somebody else, you still ultimately write for yourself. You tell whatever story it is with your personal viewpoint and you are every character you create. That is difficult to dispute so it must be true.

One other thing they all brought up is something they have all heard and they all ponder: That every story you tell is the same story told a different way. That basically, all writers have only one story to tell, one single statement to express, and that no matter how much they write, they will never get it out, and they don't even know what that story truly is. Also, too difficult to dispute.

I don't know what I'm trying to say with this and I've been writing it for almost three years, but I knew that I didn't know back when I started so I think I may be ahead of the curve, whatever that is. One thing I do know is that last run-on sentence is grammatically correct and has forty-three words.

Go ahead, Lawrence Kasdan, let's see you do that!

I might not make box office blockbusters (not yet, anyway) but I did figure out how to load that 10 minute version of BEST onto my website, so please take a look and have a few laughs.

In addition to rubbing elbows with great writers and directors, I also got to act alongside Claire Danes in the HBO movie TEMPLE GRANDIN, where she stars in the title role. I play a professor at her commencement speech.

Our Austin Filmmakers group put our second production in the can. MR. ONE NOTE was written and directed by Reagan Peterson and stars Mike Ferstenfeld, Jourdan Gibson and Leng Wong. I'll keep you updated on when and where you can catch it later.

One thing you can catch this week is my BESTest friend Darla Delgado in the TV show LIFE airing Nov 5 (Wed) at 9pm on NBC. She plays the victim whose murder they solve. Hope you can tune in or record it.

Whatever it is I'm trying to say, I hope you also open your email next month too and decide that there may be a pearl of wisdom in here that's worth plucking. It might just be that life is full of tricks and treats and that sometimes, they are one in the same.

XXXIII

The Premonition

Sent: Monday, December 1, 2008 12:03 AM
Subject: The Rembis Report - Volume XXXIII

I like to think I have perfect timing. So many times I walk into a meeting not a second too early or late but right at the split second of being on time. I like that. There are times that split second makes all the difference, and that split second has plagued me all day. I feel uncomfortably out of sync with the world. In some state of flux which has put me in the wrong place at the wrong time. Yet, here I am, safe and sound at the keyboard relating another wondrous tale for your consideration.

Strange that I should feel so out of sorts when everything went just fine and uneventful today. That is indeed what disturbs me. It could have gone wrong so quickly.

Ellen and I came back from our Thanksgiving trip to Tampa Bay today. We visited many friends and some of our favorite restaurants, beaches, and nature preserves, and then went to drive past our house. Not a house that we own or ever did own, but a little house we rented and inhabited our first year in Florida. We had a good landlord. A nice man who didn't mind that we had three cats. It was a quiet street where children played safely. We drove by and inspected the residence. It was well maintained. Trees were lush, a fresh coat of paint adorned the outside, and the old shed in back had been demolished and moved away. The house looked good. We took another moment to reminisce and we were on our way.

I waited for traffic on Clark Street. The driver I pulled behind moved stubbornly slow, so instead of taking Clark to Euclid, I cut through a side street to Dale Mabry to wait for the light across from Britton Plaza. Even before I decided to take that last turn toward Britton Plaza, where I could cross at the light, I considered taking the parallel street to Euclid, but I knew this street well, so I turned there instead, at Britton Plaza.

Sometimes I consciously recall something my father would say as we drove through the streets of Detroit. He used to say it as if spouting some silly, comical line, and said it over and over again, so that by the time I left home as a teenager, I was sick of hearing it, but would never forget it. "Green means go - ONLY when it is safe to go." he would shout. I don't know why he shouted it. Many other things went in one ear and out the other, but not this. It was one thing that actually made sense. As a result, I take care in looking both ways before I drive into traffic. Once, as a pedestrian, after I ran in front of a car and was hit because a dog chased me, I learned to look both ways on foot as well. I also learned to conquer my fear of snarling dogs (sort of).

On this trip, my friend Dave showed me his ancient film camera that shoots 120 frames per second. For those who don't know, that's fast. Extremely fast. He films archival footage for the NFL on Sundays. At the games he watches from the birds-eye of the press box and follows the journey of the football along every inch of the field as it is passed from player to player, sometimes ripped from the arms of the opponent or tossed thirty yards for a touchdown. His camera captures everything, not for instant replay, but for those slow motion moments of retrospect when they take his work and bring it back to 24 frames per second so you can see a player's fingers grasp as he stretches out to the ball and snags it from the air, or misses it completely.

It is times like these, sitting at the light at Britton Plaza, I wished I had a camera like that.

I waited. The light turned green for me. Oncoming traffic from across Dale Mabry intended to turn in either direction. To my right, a red car made a U-turn on Dale Mabry. To my left, as I inched forward, the southbound right and left lanes had cars stopped at the red light. The southbound center lane was clear. At that split second, I saw the little green car roaring toward us from the center lane. Fifty miles an hour, I guess, right through the red light. Right across my path. The oncoming traffic intending to turn halted. The red car making the U-turn narrowly escaped collision. The little green car that had run its' red light veered right past and kept going. One split second was all that was there. It was over. A close call and that was it. But in my mind, although it all happened so fast, I watched it unfold quite slowly. I observed everything in that split second and absorbed it intensely.

Malcolm Gladwell authored a book entitled BLINK. It is one of a handful of non-fiction books I have read and keep on my bookshelf. He explains this phenomenon in great detail, citing the shooting of Amadou Diallo, who was gunned down in seven seconds by police officers in the Bronx. Snap decisions and spontaneity are sometimes all that lie between life and death.

It was that careful decision to look both ways and tap the brake instead of the accelerator that made all the difference this afternoon. Yet somehow, a sense of dread has been following me all day since then. It is as if the little green car was a stern warning that I should not have been there. That I should have followed the slow driver on Clark Street. That I made a wrong turn, and although all I got out of it was a fright and a close call, I have somehow warped the fabric of time and altered my destiny. As if the universe were warning me that I made a wrong move. Now, I can't help but wonder, what did I miss? If I had gone the other way, on the road not taken, to steal a phrase, what would have happened there?

We still got to our next stop, a Mediterranean restaurant, and then the airport, now two hours early for a flight that had been delayed anyway. It made me nervous and tense because my sense of timing was now off. At least, it feels that way. Or, was I destined to get hit by that car, but somehow, strangely slowed down by the putzy driver on Clark Street?

I fell asleep on the flight to Austin. I dreamed I was talking to Tom Cruise. The only part of the conversation I can recall was Tom Cruise telling me "You're right, Mike. You're absolutely right." But right about what? I don't know. Dreams are as mysterious and probably more so than anything else there is. The only other thing I recall from the dream was that the Tom Cruise I was speaking to was his villainous character from COLLATERAL.

So I end the day with more questions than answers.

Am I somehow out of sync with the universe? Is there something I missed? Do I actually have bad timing? Or is that what you call perfect timing?

If only we could watch it all over again in slow motion. Even then, given the outcome, we would never know.

Real life can not be edited. Like this Doritos commercial we filmed for a contest. We took 30 minutes of footage and whittled it down to 30 seconds. Shot with the help of friends I met through the Austin Filmmakers group, I like to think we did a nice job.

Other editing is underway. Photographer Valerie Tamburri just refurbished her website and wants you to see it. Valerie took my headshots, and even though I couldn't find any of me on the site, it's still a nice collection of work and she's a fun gal to work with.

David Hemphill has refined his craft for the One Festival at New World School of the Arts in Miami. The dates are December 5th and 6th at 5pm and 8pm. There are eight shows in total on both days. Each show is about 20-25 minutes in length. These are written, directed, and performed by the students. This is your official invitation to his senior project performance. If you're in Miami, I would definitely encourage you to make the time to catch David. His stage presence is remarkable and you will be highly entertained.

If you can't tear yourself away from the computer, you can stay right where you are and watch THE CREED by Adam ArNali now presented in its entirety online on the Internet Movie Data Base. The Creed is about Ichiro Hattori, a Japanese Juvenile, who after finding himself trapped in a NYC basement with no recollection to how he got there, starts to recite a 14th Samurai Poem trying to inspire himself to escape before a rival African American gang comes to finish him off.

Finally, if you find yourself in Austin, you are invited to the first annual Austin Filmmakers Holiday Bash. We will screen the three films we have developed since our inception about six months ago.

Party starts at 7:00
Screenings begin at 8:00
Band at 10:00

No charge for admission.
Food and beverage available for purchase.
Come early and get a good seat.

Here's what's showing -
PEOPLE THAT DO SOMETHING
Written by Marlayna Glynn Brown
Directed by Aiah Samba

MR. ONE NOTE
Written and Directed by Reagan Peterson

GREAT ROOMMATE MANNY
Written and Directed by Jaime Orta

Meet everyone involved with each production and introduce yourself.

Have a lovely holiday no matter what you do. If you find yourself feeling out of sorts, it may just be a case of introspection that no level of analysis will ever be able to fix. You may not have perfect timing, but as long as you're not getting hurt, that's okay. Just try not to fumble the ball and everything will be fine.
Merry Christmas, Happy Hanukkah, Happy New Year!

XXXIV

Ruperto

Sent: Saturday, January 3, 2009 12:22 AM
Subject: The Rembis Report - Volume XXXIV

The accident that was looking for a place to happen found me today.

I knew it was lurking out there, waiting stealthily for a time and place to strike. My first real vehicular incident since my bumper was ripped away by a truck shortly before I left Florida. That day, I was on my way to act as Howard Bevans in PICNIC with the Players of Safety Harbor. Failure to yield was how I was cited, similar to today's incident, failure to maintain assured clear distance, no matter that the driver before me stopped rather suddenly. Nothing will be contested. I will pay the ticket and be thankful that it was not worse.

A few days after I saw the speeding car rip through the red-lit intersection at Britton Plaza, I found myself driving in a part of Austin I was less familiar with. I went under the overpass carefully and down the street to a shopping plaza. Once in my parking spot, my cell phone rang and I began a conversation with one of my clients. My vantage point gave me a view of that unfamiliar intersection a half mile away. While we spoke, I watched the traffic. Two minutes into our conversation, right where I had just driven, two SUVs collided. One of them toppled over on it's side. Dozens of other vehicles drove nearby. Witnesses stopped immediately. While we talked, I saw people rush to their aid. Surely somebody called 911. Everyone carries a cell phone. My client droned on. We discussed the pros and cons of his advertising campaign. He was unaware of what I was witnessing. Four minutes into our conversation the flashing lights of police cars blazed from every direction and blocked traffic. The vehicle on its side began to smoke. Somebody with a fire extinguisher pounced on it. Five minutes into my sales effort I saw the fire truck crew take over for the person with the extinguisher. A minute later, as I pitched the benefits of my advertising, the ambulance shot past with sirens blaring and a minute after that, I negotiated a sale and the situation a half mile away was under control.

Everything happened so fast.

Just like it did on Christmas Eve Day. On that bright and sunny day, only a mile or so from my house, I turned the corner from Giles Road onto US Highway 290 westbound toward Austin. All was typical. The light was red, the right turn lane was clear as usual and traffic was sparse, so I coasted up to the corner and made my turn. As I looked over my shoulder, to check for traffic, I saw the giant vehicle laying on its side in the ditch. Then as I focused on the undercarriage of what appeared to be a tractor trailer on its side, I saw the little 4 wheel drive Suzuki that looked like it was sitting on top of it, then, in a quick moment, I realized people were running after a white dog.

I peeled off the road and into the gas station to park. There were no police. It had just happened. I got out of the car and saw another vehicle on its side and the traffic signals laying across the road. This all happened on the other side of the road. Westbound traffic was still moving toward me. Then one police car showed up to block the eastbound intersection.

With the traffic moving toward me and the traffic signals and wires down, I studied the scene before I rushed across the two lanes of still moving traffic. Three other men jumped from a truck and ran past me defiant of the traffic, so I ran with them. Others had come on foot from other directions and surrounded the green Chevy pickup that lay on its side with a traffic signal wedged in the rear bed.

The driver was bloodied and unconscious. He was strapped inside with metal and glass crushing all around him. The shattered windshield peeled away and his Texas tag toll sticker flapped in the breeze. The nine or ten men crowded around him assessed the situation to get him out. I was an extra. Close enough to watch but not quite close enough to lend a hand. I would have been in the way.

I decided to cross the road to see if I could help with the big rig. It was not a truck, but the mother of all recreational vehicles crushed to fiberglass powder. It was towing the little Suzuki 4WD that sat on the trailer twisted behind it. The RV collapsed in the ditch. The windshield and front end were replaced by a gaping hole. Nobody appeared to be inside. People milled about nearby and another police vehicle showed up. Sirens chirped in the distance. Fire engines and paramedics came from all directions.

With nothing to do at the RV I went back to the pickup truck. They had freed the driver and we pushed the vehicle over a few inches to dislodge him. As I leaned into the roof of the truck three men pulled him out by his feet and lowered him to the other five or six below. A paramedic demanded a shirt for a pillow. One man stripped off his blue shirt to reveal his T-shirt and the crucifix that dangled from his neck and handed it to her.

Then we saw the passenger. Nobody was aware that he was buried beneath his friend everyone worked so hard to free. He was young, Mexican, with fair skin and a flannel shirt. He hung upside down. Eyes shut. Unconscious. Trapped. He was crushed from above and below with twisted steel wreckage all around him and the remnants of the deflated airbag inches from his face.

A firefighter leaned down and felt his pulse. All bystanders were concerned and offered help. "Should we push it over again?" one man asked. The firefighter told him that tools would be required. The paramedic administering aid to the man that was freed stood up and announced "All citizens who are not emergency personnel, please leave the area now." And thus our civic duty had ended.

I crossed the street and surveyed the scene trying to figure it out. I stood there a long time watching the traffic being diverted. The way they ended up on opposite sides of the street with the lights down across the road made no sense. I couldn't put it together. How did it happen? Who crossed who?

Later in the day it was the top story on the evening news. A fatal crash had closed Eastbound 290 to all traffic as officials sorted it out for several hours. The man I saw pulled from the wreckage was taken to hospital. The young man beneath him, the passenger, died at the scene. It occurred to me that I may have witnessed his final breath or the moment right after. That firefighter who checked for his pulse may have sent some subtle signal to the paramedic when he calmly told us that equipment would be needed to cut him out and she proceeded to usher us away. They knew.

I recorded the news on the other stations and watched all of the stories to piece together what might have happened. A garbage truck driver offered his eyewitness account, saying the truck tagged the back of the SUV, meaning the Suzuki in tow, and flipped over. He was the only eyewitness to get on camera. All of the reports stated that a red light had been run. When the signals hit the ground they stopped red on one side and green on the other. Some said that the truck made a U-turn into traffic. But that wouldn't make sense based on how that truck landed.

I drive through that intersection every day. Sometimes four or five times in a day. In the following days I drove slower through there and surveyed the skid marks. I looked back at the TV footage to see how the RV knocked down the light pole and how the signals landed when they smashed to the ground. Both vehicles wound up on their sides and all reports said the RV had rolled several times. Miraculously, the man and woman in the RV escaped without injury, but their two little white dogs had run off. One was killed by a car down the road and the other was not found.

The next day, only the FOX TV affiliate carried the story and reported the young man who died as 21 year old Ruperto Gardoza-Guarda. That was all they said about him. That he was 21 years old and that he died about 1:30 PM on Christmas Eve on a day where driving conditions, weather-wise, were absolutely perfect.

I searched the newspapers. I called funeral homes. I called the coroner. I thought some homage or respect should be paid to him and that perhaps I would honor him quietly at his funeral. But I never found out where it was. He was a perfect stranger. No information was out there to be had.

Although I couldn't find out more about him, I did find out one thing about the accident that was never published. When I spoke with a woman at Channel 8 she clarified the spelling of his name and told me the name of the vehicular homicide detective in charge. She asked what I saw and if I knew anything because they were looking for a third vehicle. The one that got away.

Then it all made sense. I drove home a while later and looked carefully at the intersection and the skid marks again. The pickup driver did not run the light and kill his friend as originally reported. There was another vehicle. I stood on the embankment and watched the traffic zip by. The speed limit here is 60 mph. It's easy to be going 75 when you reach this corner if your foot gets heavy.

When you make the light on the crossroad, it's easy to pass over Highway 290 at 40 mph and that light doesn't last long. A lot of people run it. Putting it all into perspective now, I can see how it happened.

Traffic flowed briskly away from Austin. Eastbound. The man and his wife in the RV were only 25 miles from their final destination on their holiday out of California minutes from seeing relatives in Elgin. Their dogs may have slept soundly or been riding along gazing at whatever it is that amuses a dog. Behind them at a relatively safe distance was the pickup truck with the two young Mexicans going about whatever business they had outside of Austin on Christmas Eve Day. The light ahead changed from red to green. Traffic was light. The RV barreled along near the speed limit, most likely, not over it. In a flash to his right, the RV driver spotted the vehicle that had disregarded the right of way, the nameless, faceless driver, had failed to yield and sped into the path of the RV. The RV driver would have slammed on his brakes to avoid the errant traveler. With the little Suzuki in tow he felt the weight shift and started to lose control. He pulled to the right to avoid the vehicle and the RV began to tilt over in the intersection and roll. The Chevy truck driver reacted, perhaps not fast enough, he may have been distracted by another vehicle, or conversation, or maybe he was moving too fast to see past the monstrous vehicle before him and he took evasive action to try and avoid the Suzuki towed by the RV. But the Suzuki must have fishtailed and caught the front end of the Chevy. As the RV slammed into the huge silver pole suspending the traffic signals the line snapped. The RV driver watched the pole disappear beneath him and the roof ripped away. The Chevy truck driver saw the giant yellow box with the glowing green light drop toward his windshield and he swerved to avoid it. He slammed on the brakes and left deep skid marks on the pavement that led into the grassy median. The light box landed on the right side of the truck bed and tipped the Chevy over making it nosedive into the ground. The airbags exploded and filled the cab with a wretched sickly gas as the windshield became a spiderweb and that was the last thing they saw.

I still do not know who Ruperto Gardoza-Guarda was. Where he was from or where he was going or what he might have become. He spent 21 years on this planet and I got to see him the moment he left. That is an odd feeling. Twenty-one years is a long time. Almost half my life. All of his.

When considering the amount of driving I do it's no wonder I get into accidents and collect a ticket now and again. When I ponder it further I think how lucky I am to be alive, considering all of the roads I have traveled and especially where I have been in the last 21 years, just to make a point of measure. Most of that time I was not the passenger. I am beginning to think that that is the point. It's not about being the passenger - watching life go by. It's about being the driver - the person in control of your own destiny. Although any slight distraction may drag you off course, sometimes, a slight moment can alter the course of your life in a devastating way, but you may be able to pick up the pieces and move on again and be ever stronger for doing so. Being the passenger scares me more - to only be along for the ride. While a driver has the option of making decisions, right or wrong, that is a freedom the passenger will never know.

And now for the news.

The good people at Doritos are giving us a second chance to

unlock our potentials and announced an extension for submissions for their Super Bowl Commercial contest. We took ours back to the editing room and came up with what we feel is a better, crunchier version and hope you will take a look at IT MATTTERS. I know it's spelled with 3 T's. The first version only had 2 and I typoed as I resubmitted. If you would be so kind as to pass along the link to all of your family and friends who love tasty chips or football or both, you may be eligible to win a trip to Super Bowl XLIII in 2010 simply for casting your vote for It Mattters, because it really does.

Here's one more act of shameless self promotion, just to let you know what else I've been up to. I co-wrote a movie that is now in development with Green Pictures and Streetwise Productions. UNPUNISHED tells the story of Carla Ruiz and her search for her missing sister in Juarez Mexico. This film has finally validated my writing as an art form and I now have my first IMDB writing credit.

From The Response File
Volume XXXIV

Received: Thursday, January 8, 2008 8:06 PM
Mike,
I just found this in my "Drafts" folder and am left wondering if I ever sent it to you? (It would have been on the same day you sent your Volume XXXIV.) And if I did, please forgive the "reduncedancy" and know that this is not an attempt to fish for any feedback on it.

Wow...that was really interesting, Mike. I read it moments after sending you my favorable and unsolicited comment about your acting. But you can write, too! Who knew? (Just kidding.)

In all seriousness, though, the recounting of both your 1/2-mile-away observation while servicing a client, and the immersive description of the RV/pick-up accident were quite vivid and rang emotionally true. It immediately reminded me of an ongoing "project-in-my-head" that started exactly two years ago.

My wife, Marsha and I were heading back home from Downtown's second "First Night" celebration New Year's Eve (12.30AM on Jan 1,2007). Just upstream the short stretch of southbound MoPac Expressway between Hwy 360 and Southwest Parkway traffic suddenly came to a halt. "Must be an accident up there," I said to her.

After a long "impromptu parking lot experience" which lasted about 10 minutes, we were motioned to move ahead by a peace officer standing on the shoulder.

"Yikes, when so many official vehicles are on a scene...and yep, there's a coroner's van...somebody died." I said to Marsha. As we crawled by the scene, I peered into the maze of flashing lights and personnel scattered down the gently sloping embankment to our right and got a solid glimpse at the crashed vehicle. "Oh shit!" I gasped, stunned at what was the most accordioned car I had ever seen. The older Japanese import had literally wrapped its entire front end around an oak tree, and it looked like the rest of the chassis had caught up in a hurry. There was no way anyone could have survived having the engine and passenger compartments trade places like that.

Seeing the twisted metal alone was shocking enough, and thankfully there was nothing else to see.

In the following days, and now months and years, I found myself occasionally preoccupied with this incident. A couple of days later, I pulled off the freeway and walked down to the crash-site. The car was gone of course, but I walked around fascinated by the forensic evidence. The mighty oak had sustained a bit of bark stripping, it may have leaned more than a few days earlier, but it did not snap, it absorbed (or I should say the car did) the entire force of the impact. Several yards past the tree I found the heating control cluster for the Toyota...it had been cleanly separated from the rest of the dashboard. That was kind of chilling.

Walking further past the tree, I began to find more of the car's interior parts scattered around, like the gear-shift knob and rear-view mirror. I sure hope the car's occupant(s) died instantly.

Another couple of days later, I drove past that same spot after work and saw a couple of cars pulled off to the side of the highway nearby. Three or four people had congregated at the crash site.

Family no doubt. The next day I made the same stop. Golden central Texas afternoon winter light shone upon the dry beige grass carpeting the embankment, broken only by the two gouged skid marks from the long gone accordion vehicle.

At the bottom of the hill, propped up against the freshly scarred oak was a makeshift cross and a bundle of yellow-white roses. In the center of the cross was a photo of Benito Z. the 19 year-old boy-man who died. He looked really high in the picture, with a beer on one hand and a big old slit-eyed goofy grin on his face.

Here he was loved. But maybe he was the last to know it.

I paid my respects to the Benito I only posthumously knew. It just seemed so sudden, to be driving (between parties?) at midnight and never see the New Year's Day you're celebrating. To skip off the road diagonally down a gentle embankment and be abruptly stopped by a tree. Completely stopped.

I tried to understand how it could have happened that way. In Benito's benefit of the doubt, I think he tried to miss rear-ending a car that had suddenly braked in front of him for whatever reason. A slight steering correction and off the asphalt he went.

Two years later, I still think of his passing. In fact I give respect to him, and the oak tree nearly every time I drive by the spot. I was going to leave a note of condolence to the family on the memorial marker this New Year's Eve, but I never got around to it. I'm sure the family has enough heartache without having some gringo stranger wax off about "The Benito he never knew" or some horse-effluvia like that.

But I'm grateful you gave me the opportunity to write about it at long last.

Peace, and safer driving,
Radames Pera

XXXV

Home

Sent: Sunday, February 1, 2009 12:47 PM
Subject: The Rembis Report - Volume XXXV

I travel so much.

In the past month I have resided in hotel rooms in Denver, Dallas, Boston, and Las Vegas. I can't tell you anything about Las Vegas, because, in case you haven't heard, what happens there, stays there.

There is a Deju Vu type of sensation I get sometimes. Most frequent travelers have experienced this at some point, waking up, and not knowing where you are. That happened to me recently. Nothing in particular woke me up, I just did. The darkness enveloped me and my nearsighted eyes, blurred by the absence of my glasses, could only discern light peeking from the edge of the window and the warm glow of the alarm clock. For what felt like a few minutes, I could not remember where I was. I reached where I normally keep my glasses when I sleep, on the floor, beneath the bed, finding only carpet and baseboards. I was lost. I held the clock up and squinted to find a wee morning hour ticking past. But where, what time zone? I felt my glasses on the nightstand and flicked on the light in the room. It looked like a hotel I stayed in last year, in Romulus Michigan, but no, wait. This is . . . this is . . . Boston. It really took more time than I was comfortable with to cognitively focus on my surroundings and know where I was. If time travel were possible, I imagine that feeling when you arrive must be akin to this.

It takes a few minutes to get back to sleep when the sensation is powerful like that. Stranger yet, is what happened to me a few nights ago. I woke up the same way, not knowing where I was. This time I realized that I truly did not know where I was. Ambient light shafted in from the corners of the windows and door frame, but this was a room I didn't recall entering to begin with, and this time, I could not find my glasses. I stood up to survey my surroundings better and turn on a light. With the next momentary survey, the room came into focus, but I could find none of my luggage, or anything to indicate that I had spent a great deal of time in that atypical hotel room. Then I figured it out. I was dreaming.

Later, in the morning, when I did wake up in my own bed at home, with my dear, sweet wife Ellen by my side, I knew where I was and I was comforted. There was no longer a sense of disconnection to the world around me. But of course, I do not shake this dream easily. It makes me wonder about the next time I do wake up in a hotel room, not knowing where I am. How long will that hazy disconnection last next time?

There is something eerily enthralling about it. As if the world is a clean slate and you can walk out that hotel room door into a place where not just anything can happen, but you can make anything happen. For the time between waking and hearing any other sign of life I am free to imagine anything I wish. Once you turn on the TV to the Today Show or walk into the hallway and the maids greet you with "Good morning, sir." that imaginary world comes to an end and life goes on as you know it to be.

I bid farewell to my friends at The Austin Filmmakers last week. Travis McAllister came from the other side of the room and told me he *"Felt disconnected over there."* The conversation only paces away had not included him. It was good for him to come over to speak with us. His presence now and commitment to keeping involved diluted the memories I had of him not showing up for a shoot when he said he would. Things happen, he is young, and another chance to show his talent is not out of the question. He wants to stay connected. That is a good thing.

That is why I write this every month. To stay connected.

I had a strange holiday this year. Besides seeing the young Mexican man crushed to death on Christmas Eve Day, I spent the holiday without Ellen. Our personal circumstances pulled us apart and we were disconnected. Our pets searched for her when she was gone. They do the same when I leave town. The dog waits at the window and the cats look in closets hoping to find me.

When I went up to Dallas I visited with the Fort Worth Television and Film Production Meetup Group just to make a connection. Much like The Austin Filmmakers were when we started, they had ideas and talent to share but not enough to work with yet, but they will get there.

Being a part of the group, connecting with people, is what these meetups are all about. What is amazing about it is how it can pull you in such a way that you are then disconnected from another part of your life. Social networking is a relatively new term that was not truly discussed 20 years ago. Now, being able to find people to meet and things to do via the Internet, it becomes an entirely new platform on which to build relationships. All the while, for some, building those connections can help to disintegrate the real ones that already exist. I have killed my MySpace and Facebook pages. They no longer exist. I found the time I was spending there not only could have been put to better use writing fiction, but in effect, disconnected me from my real life.

Don't get the idea that I am blaming the Internet for anything, I'm not. This is merely an observation. Without the Internet, you would never get the Rembis Report, and I know you wouldn't want to do without that.

My work now will keep me on the road. A new or familiar city every week. Next week, I go back to Salt Lake City, Utah, where Ellen and I lived during the mid 1990's. After that Chicago, where I ran off to for my first vacation alone when I was 14. Then Atlanta, where I have never spent more than a few hours passing through.

With all of these cities on my calendar, and Austin not feeling like the home we hoped it would be, we now turn full circle and in two weeks will move back to Clearwater, only a block away from where we lived three years ago. Our tenure in Austin will equate to exactly one year to the day we arrived.

I did make some connections in Austin, good ones, and it will always be a place where I felt like I was accomplishing something, but not a place I intend to come back to, not for more than a visit, maybe someday.

Florida is our home. Ellen informed me in 1999 when we first got to Tampa that she was told that Florida meant "Full of Flowers". In the last three years the closest we have come to having a home full of flowers was our garden in Billings which only bloomed from May until September. Our yards in Livingston and Austin were desolate. Now we will go where flowers bloom all year long. A place we feel connected.

I contemplate ending the Rembis Report now. I have shared with you dozens of observations over the last 36 months and I know that in my first issue I said I would relay my messages for 24. I do not want to overstay my welcome, or become stale. Perhaps I will write to you again in a few months.

I'd like to end on a high note. BEST has finally been recognized by the Internet Movie Data Base as a film. I feel that I can return to Florida with a great deal of pride not only for this, but for the success of my other screenplays and short films. I also plan to reconnect with my many friends there and work on bigger and better projects.

In two weeks I will be driving a U-Haul truck with everything we own back home. Ellen will have our pets in the car and we will ride in tandem. I am going to watch for the green sign on the side of Interstate 10 that reads Tallahassee 144 (miles) somewhere around Pensacola. I stood next to that sign for 9 hours once on my very first trip to Orlando with a bearded man named Bruce. We were both hitchhiking. I don't know where Bruce was going. Finally, after waiting all day, two guys in a crumby, rusty old Cadillac picked us up. At one time this car with the big back seat was a luxury vehicle. Now it served to chauffeur two poor travelers part way home.

Home. That is where we are going.

The next time you wake up in an unfamiliar haze, as the world around you shifts into view, may you not be lost. May you be home.

Fare Well

From The Response File
Volume XXXV

Received: Saturday, February 14, 2009 10:52 AM
"I have killed my My Myspace and Facebook pages. They no longer exist. I found the time I was spending there not only could have been put to better use writing fiction, but in effect, disconnected me from my real life."

Thank you. Write, create, and be free of the fake bullshit. Good old fashioned real communication. (Of course, this being said through email, that irony does not escape me....)

I have not read the rest of your email. Perhaps it will say that you will no longer communicate this way so this shall be lost in the wind...

Maureen

The Response File

The Response File

Volume I

Received: Saturday, April 01, 2006 9:19 AM
Oh my ... what a surprise .... you're moving to Montana!!!!!?????!!!!!?????
Wow!!!!
I wish you and your wife all the best.
It has been really nice knowing and working with you.
Vicki Wayne

Received: Saturday, April 01, 2006 9:26 AM
Hi Mike
I am so happy to have met you and acted with you, I believe that people always come into our lives for a reason, even if only a brief moment. I doubt I will ever be in Montana, but hopefully our paths will cross again. I am planning to audition for Coffee, so I'll let you know what happens with that. Lots of luck with your move.
Peace, Angy (Flo)

Also wanted to let you know my son Dan is in the production business in Orlando, maybe you can send him a copy of BEST.

Angy

Received: Saturday, April 01, 2006 9:30 AM
Bon Voyage Mike!
I wish you all the best out in the wild west.
Are you coming to the "Waste of Space" wrap party tonight?
-Tom

Received: Saturday, April 01, 2006 10:49 AM
Well Mike (or is it John Denver?),
Take care of yourself. I enjoyed knowing you. Montana is a beautiful state. I look forward to your monthly missives.
Walter Raine

Received: Saturday, April 01, 2006 11:25 AM
Hi, Don't let the door hit you in the ass on your way out! LOL! Are you keeping the same email? Good luck to you guys.
LM

Received: Saturday, April 01, 2006 11:40 AM
i love the rembis report! can't wait to here all about your adventures. we'll keep you in touch with ours as well. sorry to hear about your neighbor. that's terrible. the lesson: love everyday, right?

have a safe trip and i can't wait to saddle up and ride some trails with you in montana!!

-scott

Received: Saturday, April 01, 2006 12:23 PM
Sounds like you're going to have a busy and full future, Mike. All the best, and watch out for the bears out there.
Ab Morgan

Received: Saturday, April 01, 2006 12:53 PM
Godspeed, Mike and Ellen.
Khoury

Received: Saturday, April 01, 2006 2:12 PM
Just when I think I have lost touch with all of my acting buddies, I receive this! I will write more at another time but just wanted to wish you and your wife all of the best. I expect to hear great things about you someday Mike Rembis. Don't give up. You have given me inspiration to keep moving forward with acting and as soon as I finish with graduate school will definitely put more of an effort into it.
Take Care of yourself,
Missy Escribano

Received: Sunday, April 02, 2006 11:50 PM
Dearest Mike,
How charming I found your correspondence [did I spell that right?] What the hell are ya doing? Didn't you know that's where they filmed Brokeback Mountain? Are you nuts? or do you like nuts? I'm glad you included me in your letters. You were the only one who thought pretty much on the same brain wave as myself about that job. That's really showing Mitch huh? You can't fire me cuz I'm moving asshole. I wish you well out there, I'm sure It's beautiful. Please send me pictures and if you get a chance you should try looting an archaeological site, I personally love it. I'm currently scouting a burial mound I found out in Ft. Lonesome off of the Alafia River.

The only thing I've found so far is a moonshine still from the 1940's. I've sent some pictures of my boy fishing on the river. My friend from church has 1000 acres in Ft. Lonesome he runs cattle on. The river runs through his property also there are 4 spring fed creeks that run into the river. Anyway this isn't about me it's about you and your wife. I wish ya'll the best on your journey.

your country friend, Jeff

Received: Monday, April 03, 2006 9:37 AM

Hey Mike!! I am so sorry to hear you are leaving us!!! When I saw your email in my inbox my first thought was, "I need to pay him a visit!" But I guess if I do that I'll be going to Montana? lol. That's so exciting though and I must say I am a bit jealous. I've always wanted to head out west and herd cattle across Montana or Colorado or Wyoming....some cool place like that. :O) A dream job....though it may never happen.

Glad to hear BEST is still out there reaching people's funny bone and trying for success. Don't give up!! You have a great talent and an awesome sense of humor!!

If you ever need anything from Florida don't hesitate to ask....pictures of palm trees, shells, sand. I don't think I can box up the heat but I could try. ;O) Please have a safe trip. All the best to you and Ellen. Working with you two was truly the most fun I've had in this business. God bless and keep in touch.

Molly

PS: When I'm melting my ass off in the summer heat and my shoes are glued to the pavement....I'll think of you, enjoying the cool summer of Montana. BUT...when you're freezing your ass off in the snow and slipping on icy sidewalks....think of us down in Florida, sipping pina coladas on the beach. ;O) Hey at least you won't have hurricanes!! lol. We'll miss you guys!!! Take care!!

Received: Monday, April 03, 2006 11:20 AM
hey mikey,
welcome back to Montana, I hope it's better for you than it's been for me.. Since I've been here I've lost thousands of dollars...
peace
kev
_.

Received: Monday, April 03, 2006 11:24 AM
MIKE, I WILL MISS YOU!!!!!!
TILISIA

Received: Tuesday, April 04, 2006 9:26 AM
Hi Mike:
I was very sad to hear that you and your wife are leaving the area, and moving back to Montana of all places. Doug and I lived in Great Falls for about 9 months when he was in the Air Force. It was an interesting experience for newlyweds from Pensacola, FL. The year we were there (1967-1968) it snowed on the 4th of July. We joke and say "there are 2 seasons in Montana...winter and August!" It was an interesting place that I would love to see again through more mature eyes.

Continue your journey with Best and your other projects...this move may be just what you need...who knows. Best of luck to you. It's been great working with you. Let me know how things are progressing.
Sue

Received: Friday, April 07, 2006 1:18 AM
Wow Mike.
I remember the first time I met you I walked into Corinne's class

and there you were. The first thing that struck me was your booming voice. I really envy your projection and I actually use your sound in my head sometimes to get me to project.

I loved working on Breast Men with you. I wish we could have performed it together. But, all of a sudden I did three straight shows over the past seven months and it has just flown by.

So much is happening right now it baffles me to look back at the last six months and take it in as well.

Even though I've only known you eight or ten months, I always felt like I've always known you and have been really comfortable around you.

I do see your crazy side and I think you are a driven and talented writer, that's a great combination for success. Your stride is picking up momentum, keep pushing, I think you're going to breakthrough big.

Remember my part.

Anytime you ever get a gig where you need to come film here for two weeks or a month, you can stay at my place for free.

I'm glad you feel like your accomplishments here have been many. You seem excited about moving and sentimental about leaving.

I know, it's tough to leave a family. The acting world is a struggling, working, myriad-of-people, from-all-walks-of-life, family/support-group.

You know you're gonna be back here soon for a festival or something.

Life is a crazy journey, you fit right in.

You're a good person and you spread laughter, love and happiness.

I Thank you for having me on your list.

I know we'll see each other again, I'm in the bizz for the long-haul,

so, I'm staying plugged-in. Break a Leg out there in Montana. Where the hell is Montana anyway?
Ronald

Received: Friday, April 14, 2006 7:31 PM
Hey Mike and Ellen

I guess you are in Montana now, and totally tired of hearing the song of "cats in the car." Although they probably settled down once they understood that they were not headed to the vet.

Just sending you some love and hope you are settling in well. Feed Chris when he arrives, I think he may be tired of "road food." Sounded like he was having a blast though. Talked to him when he was going through the badlands, playing "renegade" or "stage coach robber" or "man on the run." I think his imagination got the best of him, but that is so cool.

LOL
Keep in touch and stay happy.
Corinne

Received: Tuesday, April 25, 2006 9:50 AM
Hi Mike:

I'm sure people like you can find whatever they want whenever they live. You are this kind of person who enjoys everything and can see all the little details life offers to us.

I'm sure you will be very happy with this change and I'm going to miss you because I knew all your professional skills too late.

Good luck and.....be careful with the bears!!!!
Bianca

Volume II

Received: Monday, May 1, 2006 12:51 PM
Hey Mike!!!!

I do enjoy your stories. They truly are entertaining. I am so sorry I have not yet called. I keep meaning to, but then I get distracted. I am horrible with the phone, but pretty good with the email. The girls miss you over here. It's funny how you feel differently when someone is far away. When you were here, we knew we could see you anytime, so it was okay, now that you're gone, we know we can't and we'd like to see you more often. Well enough of that (your heads probably big now), I just wanted to let you know you are thought of fondly and missed.

I wish you all the luck in the acting circuit over there. As for me, I am losing weight and I am getting back to auditioning for movies. I started my diet and exercise program last Sunday 4/23 and as of today I have lost 6 pounds! I wasn't auditioning as much because I was feeling as though they don't really want to see the cute real woman body, they want to see the skinny mini body, so I got discouraged for a little while, but now I am back. I'm doing Weight Watchers. I feel great! I have lots of energy and I still get to eat what I want! That truly is my kind of diet =P.

Well, I am glad all is well, and keep doing what you are doing.
Annette

Received: Monday, May 1, 2006 1:12 PM
Enjoyed your "report." Mike. I assume you've considered turning it into a screenplay; it might be fun! I truly love the West, having lived in California for several years. I grew up in Indiana & Michigan, but at least they are west of the East and north of the South! Whatever, "it's a small world." Thanks for keeping in touch.

By the way, I was working with a children's theater group at the Venue who put on a play called "The Party Pig."

The sad thing was that the children were not allowed to oink!

Best wishes, Kathleen

Received: Monday, May 1, 2006 11:12 PM
Cool Mike. Thanks for the update breast man. Keepem comin. I wouldn't mind taking a trip back to the 50s.
Ronald

Received: Tuesday, May 2, 2006 7:26 PM
Hi Mike and Ellen,

Glad you made it out West safely. Do they have Moose burgers out there? I think I'd dig a Moose burger ... with cheese.

Good to hear you're in the hunt for the film fest.

What did you submit?

I just got back online after a 3 month hiatus so hit me with any news I may have missed.

out for now,
Tim

Received: Wednesday, May 3, 2006 9:42 PM
hey Mikey,
nice recapp of the journey whatz yer number
406 222 ????
peace
going to my fair lady with jess
she's six months pregnant
whoa
peace
kev

Volume III

Received: Thursday, June 1, 2006 6:39 AM
WHAT KIND OF WEED DO THEY GROW OUT THERE!!!
Please send me some..........LM

Received: Thursday, June 1, 2006 8:30 AM
Hello there Mike,

I am so happy that you are doing well and still keeping yourself in the business. I'm doing pretty good myself, as I lost 15 pounds and feel more like my old self again. Ryan is doing good at his job, for right now, but we are trying to get him in a more suitable job for him. This is just income for right now. Anyway, as for your idea, I think you need to write out a very detailed plan of action for this. It would cost a lot of money, but if you swing it the right way, then maybe you would be able to get the hotel to pay for it. Unless that was your plan all along. I know actors usually work for cheap, but we are talking long hours here and always on, so I think that alone should be $1000 a day. Now I might be crazy, but that sounds about right to me. Let me know what everyone else thinks.

Annette

Received: Thursday, June 1, 2006 12:59 PM
Mike

Good idea on the theme park. They do actually do the same thing in Tombstone, Arizona, and every day they re-enact the gunfight at the O.K. Corral. If you could link a piece of history to the town about something famous that happened there, it could become a landmark event and tourists would come from everywhere to see it. There was a sequel to Westworld. I can't remember the name of it though.

Ronald

Received: Friday, June 2, 2006 8:36 PM
Mike,

You always have a way with words. I look forward to every Rembis Report.

As for me, I work a lot in music videos these days. You can view some videos that I have directed at Somepicnic.com and other videos that I have worked on at MySpace.com/thefilmcore (I was director of photography on the Run Kid Run video, and did lighting on the Baumer, Dave Melillo, As I Lay Dying, Cannibal Corpse and Dead Man Running clips, I also worked on the Spoken and Horse The Band "Birdo" Video).

Work in LA is hard to come by. That was a lie. I've worked on so much, and I've only been here for 9 months. I haven't had to get a dreaded "regular" job yet. I'm also wrapping up the editing on a video for Nonpoint that I directed. My 1st major label video!

Say hello to your wife for me. She's the best craft service woman ever. I hope you guys make it out here someday, or better yet, make a movie where you're at now. A dramatic/comedic piece on a place in the middle of Montana. You probably won't have to pay for a damn thing there. I recommend joining MySpace to meet people in your area that are interested in film. I get most of my work in LA because I befriend someone on MySpace. Just so happens that he was an intern of one of my heroes as far as music videos go. Now he produces for him. I work with them all the time. They even sent me to do that major label video. Unfortunately, I'm too old for pedophiles, so I haven't met any of them on myspace. You win some, you lose some.

Keep the reports coming. Later.
Mario.

Received: Sunday, June 4, 2006 4:21 PM
Hi Mike,
How's this for a small world? I looked through your list of people who you sent this message to. Apparently we know a lot of the same talented individuals. There are a few I'm sure you can name offhand, but see the list gets bigger. I just did a play called "A Few Good men." That means I became familiar with John Benincasa (director) Maureen Smithorbob, Parker Dowling, and Ronald Farnham.

Oh yeah, that's a helluva story.

D.D.

Received: Monday, June 5, 2006 5:03 PM
Hey Mike,
Congrats and more Congrats..sounds like things are moving right along with you...and I am so keeping my mouth shut about the theme park...I'm giggling as I type this...too funny!!! Hugs

Junia

Received: Thursday, June 8, 2006 10:56 PM
Hey Mike,
Nice report. Can I get that with a side of bacon? :)

Sounds like you're getting settled in up there. Congrats on making the finals on the screenplay contest.

Say...can you change my e-mail address to this one? I rarely, if ever check that one you have. All you have to do is change the "_" (underscore) to a "-" (hyphen) in the one you already have. The correct e-mail is this one you're reading.

Thanks man. Keep up the good work.

Best regards,

Russell Hess

Actor/Producer/Writer

"Press on. Nothing can take the place of persistence. Talent will not;

the world is full of unsuccessful people with talent. Genius will not; unrewarded genius is almost a proverb. Education alone will not; the world is full of educated derelicts. Persistence and determination alone are omnipotent." - Calvin Coolidge[11]

Received: Friday, June 9, 2006 11:09 AM
I finally had the time to read!! Congrats to you Mikey!!!!
I wish you good luck. Keep me posted with Blondzilla up dates! Also, did Dave talk to you regarding doing some adjustments to Steve O yet? I know he wanted to talk to you about that!
P.S. Thanks for the info on car rentals. I'm gonna check out cars this weekend! Thanks!!!!
jilly

Volume IV

Received: Saturday, July 1, 2006 7:35 AM
Maybe you should open a Chinese restaurant next to the car wash. It sounds like there's a large supply of free meat for your menu............LM

Received: Saturday, July 1, 2006 11:19 AM
Mike,
It's good to hear that life is good for you. I really enjoyed your nature stories (I have a soft spot for animals).
Your writing style in this e-mail has that Garrison Keillor sort of tender, down home, quaint, warm-fuzzy feel to it. You might consider creating a radio show or even compiling your writings, like this one, into a book...Your e-mail letters are not the typical "read and run" type e-mails. I actually had a few minutes, so when I saw your e-mail I went and made my cup of coffee, so I could take my time, sip my coffee, and sit and enjoy reading.

Thanks for sharing...
Priscilla

My Reply:
Thanks Priscilla, I sort of feel *Keillorish* when I am writing. I'm glad you like the report. Psst! Keep this a secret. The Rembis Report IS a book. Or at least I intend for it to be in the end. Each month is a chapter. How will it end? I don't even know.
Take Care, Mike
Publishing this book was only an idea then. Never certain it would happen, I wrote every letter with this in mind, just in case.

Priscilla's Reply:
Go for it! Good for you. What a great way to discipline yourself to set a goal to create on a regular basis! Great idea!
Take care, Priscilla

Received: Saturday, July 1, 2006 1:03 PM
Thanks for the news Mike. Always nice to hear.
Re photo of bison and elk, just like you to get an ass shot! LOL
Sounds like you are having fun with ducks and skunks, but stay away from the skunks. And learn Cantonese when you next go to China.
Venue is having some good camps. Comedy this week was excellent, but Tony Gaud became ill last week (in the middle of Comedy Camp 1) on a commercial set, his BP was up to 200 and last I knew he was still in the hospital undergoing tests.
We have a week off (I need it) then come back with a TV camp and a
Musical camp "Chicago" in July.
Stray Dogs will be bringing in their play "Extremities" in Sept/Oct, and

we will be doing "Jewel Thieves" Oct/Nov.
Busy. Trying to survive, looking for a new space again.
Love to you and Ellen.
Corinne

Received: Sunday, July 2, 2006 8:07 AM
Hey Mike
Good to hear from you. Just had a birthday on Friday. Carolyn is bringing her grandson to the beach today to hang out.

I've had a rough time with Coung the past few weeks. I'm pretty sure it is over between us. He has moved out all his clothes. He finished off my house while I was out with my neighbor. My house looks fabulous.

My sister is coming to visit next weekend on their way back from a cruise.

Work is work.
Good to hear from you.
Susan

My reply:
Hi Susan,
Sorry for your heartache. What do you mean he finished off your house? You mean, fixing it up, construction wise? We have painted and wallpapered most of our upstairs living area and we have to rip out these carpets. The previous owners were smokers and it STILL smells like smoke. I thought the paint would make it go away.

HAPPY BIRTHDAY!!!!!!!!!!!!!! I'll mark my calendar so I don't miss the next one.

Work is great here. Customers are about the same and the attorneys are the same as you get down there. But the people I work with are all SO nice. It's really fun to be with them. Our boss is normal and easy to talk to. I really do work it the way I want to. I am mentoring a new employee this month. The volume of sales actually gives me about the same paycheck I have been used to in Florida. We closed out Billings last week and I had 12 sales.

I'll give you a call soon.

Mike

Susan's Reply:

Yes, fixing up the house. Closet Doors, painted the bedrooms etc. Sounds like you have been busy fixing up.

I'm glad you like the people you work with. Lisa and I have been hanging out a little. She is actually a really cool individual. Linda is still complaining. Ha ha Mitchell it seems has eased up a little.

Have a happy 4th of July

Susan

Volume V

Received: Monday, July 31, 2006 10:27 PM

Had a terrible storm on Saturday and did not drive to Tarpon Springs. But I called them and this lovely lady called me back today to say their power went out so I can use my tickets this weekend which I will do, I have to call her and let her know which show. Probably Saturday, but I am still looking for a date, I will have to advertise on the Vennet! LOL

What think you of Verizon on line yellow pages.

I was approached today.

Love the Rembis Report.

Corinne

Received: Monday, July 31, 2006 10:34 PM

Are you a travel agent?

Received: Monday, July 31, 2006 11:29 PM
Mike

Dude you're funny. You will write a sitcom about what's going on in that part of the country. There is so much untapped humor there; and with the popularity of Napoleon Dynamite, you know it will sell. I know you would much rather write, direct, act, produce, and be a part of that life than selling advertisement. I know, it takes time. I tell myself the same thing every time I swipe my badge into SOCOM. We'll meet on the red carpet someday.

Ronald

Received: Tuesday, August 1, 2006 8:00 AM
Hey Mike,

It's Vicki Wayne ...... yeah, I know it's been a long time.

I just have to tell you, I really enjoy reading your reports. You certainly do have a way of painting pictures with words. As I was reading I saw everything you described. Beautiful.

I'd love to see that part of the country.

It sounds like things are going well for you. I'm very happy for you. I wish you the best.

I've got to run for now.

Take care.

Vicki

Received: Tuesday, August 1, 2006 9:38 AM
You are too funny!!
Pam Rush

Received: Thursday, August 3, 2006 8:53 AM
Hi, You need therapy! I'm here for you......LM

Volume VI

Received: Friday, September 1, 2006 2:26 PM
Cool report. Break a leg.

Received: Friday, September 1, 2006 4:34 PM
Don't forget! Smoking the stuff you smoke and drinking the amount you do, you only have 42 working brain cells.
LM

Received: Friday, September 1, 2006 8:15 PM
How funny, Mike! And, Happy Birthday! You are a very clever writer. Cheers, Kathleen Mc. (Aunt Abby)

Received: Saturday, September 2, 2006 8:59 AM
Hey Michael
It's always good to hear from you and read your stories. You are a very good writer. I'm sure one of the scripts you have written will hit the big time.
Life is good here. We missed the last hurricane Ernesto. Can't wait for some cooler weather.
I rescued a dog last Saturday. A 4 year old Chihuahua. I named her Lucy. She is really cute. We are working on the potty training. But she is a sweetheart.
Have a great weekend.
Susan

Received: Saturday, September 2, 2006 10:18 AM
Happy Birthday. I turn 44 this month!! I think we'll survive.
Pam Rush

Volume VII

Received: Sunday, October 1, 2006 2:06 PM
Hi Mike

Thanks for COFFEE, I love it, and know i have a copy somewhere, but my filing system is a mess.

I am glad that you are involved with a theatre. This looks like a good producing group and I hope that you stay with it.

I am going to refer to your statement *"This much rehearsal creates an internal music shuffle that also includes snippets of dialogue. I don't even think about my lines before I walk on stage, as I have in the past, they just happen. I have become a robotic singing actor that delivers everything on cue."*

Actually, Mike, that is called being in the moment. You no longer have to "think" about it, you do it and NOW you can apply all of the "acting" stuff you learned, subtext, etc.

Hey, you have made an enormous breakthrough.

Thanks for the creepy man story. Very funny. How did they receive YOUR poem, you never said. Perhaps the host will learn to do things on tape and then broadcast after she can edit. Perhaps she will invite you back again, so those who turned off the show will listen to yours. LOL

Love to you both.
Corinne

Received: Monday, October 2, 2006 11:51 AM
I heard there are huge deposits of uranium in Montana.........LM

Received: Monday, October 2, 2006 12:34 PM
Greetings, Mike!

Thank you so much for the "Coffee" poem! It already did have influence on me; I had to go get another cup of coffee while reading it. How clever! I think that next year, instead of putting milk & cookies out for Santa, I'll brew him a cup of coffee. Seriously, I assume that you have a copyright for it? Very clever!!!

"Man of La Mancha" is a wonderful play. They're going to do it at the Francis Wilson next year, and I hope to be involved in it. I'm currently in the Gilbert & Sullivan musical, "Ruddigore." The Lary Awards were last night, and I saw lots of folks there. I just wish that community theater paid!!!

Bravo! Kathleen (Aunt Abby)

Received: Tuesday, October 3, 2006 4:53 PM
Hey Mike,
So sorry its taken me awhile to reply to your email and phone call. I am so happy for you, that you recited your poem on the radio. It must of been a thrill to do, even if your fellow poets were a little creepy. I am very proud of you for still doing your thing over there. I wish I could see you in that play, I am sure you are great. If anyone records it by chance, please send a tape/DVD our way.

Not doing a whole lot on my end. I am still working at HSN at all hours of the night. I got a part in this Fan film of Star Wars, but they haven't started shooting yet, and I don't know if its going to happen or not. We will see. Darla has one of the female leads in the film. There was also some talk about another movie that I am guaranteed a role in if its ever done, but that might have fallen through also. So basically there are a lot of maybes going on for me right now.

Ryan is doing well. I don't know if you know or not, but he is working for my uncle with satellite and E-911. He basically tests the 911 calls of cellular phones, so he travels a lot. He's home right now, but I believe he will be leaving on Friday. Well that's my story. Keep up the good work with acting.

Annette

Received: Friday, October 6, 2006 6:20 AM
Hi Mike;

Great poem. but I don't think I could remember all of it. I should send you the poem I wrote about my mother who passed away almost 22 years now. I still think of her often.

Going up to Canada tomorrow for Thanks Giving, so the turkeys we do not eat we send down to the USA for their Thanks Giving a month later.

Take Care
Sonny

Volume VIII

Received: Thursday, November 2, 2006 10:39 AM
Mike: I hope you know how much I enjoy your e-mails and especially the pictures. Thanks for keeping me on your list. It makes me want to move to the mountains - The Smokeys though, not Montana!

Pam Rush

Received: Thursday, November 2, 2006 7:09 PM
Interesting report, Mike. And some nice photos too! Since you obviously like photography, are you interested in a couple of excellent professional 35mm cameras? I used to be a pro photographer, but have stopped - so I can give you a good deal on some stuff. Let me know.

Also - I didn't know you were going to do "Man of La Mancha"! Did you know that I did that on Broadway, and was on the first National Tour of it for three years? I understudied "Sancho" and performed it many times. What part did you play? Dr. Carrasco?

I've also directed it a couple of times. When you come back, I'll show you some photos.

Take care - stay warm - and God Bless!

Victor

Received: Thursday, November 2, 2006 8:14 PM

My fingers are crossed for you. You are so talented, I know it will happen for you!:)

I guess for now I won't keep whining about the cold front coming through bring us 40 & 50 degree weather.....

Missy

Received: Friday, November 3, 2006 3:01 AM

My videos are getting some airplay on myspace. I dedicated one of the pages to the beginning of Best. I sent it out as a bulletin to over 1000 people.

Jeff Crabtree

Received: Sunday, November 5, 2006 9:06 PM

Very beautiful pictures. Thanks for the update. Try and stay warm. I wish you the best with BEST.

My dog Lucy is getting cuter every day. She is really a great dog. Time for bed.

Susan

Volume IX

Received: Friday, December 1, 2006 2:37 PM
Mike,

I just want you to know that although I never reply, I thoroughly enjoy reading your emails. You should compile these little gems and make a book out of them eventually.

Happy Holidays from sunny/rainy/hot/cool Florida.

Deanna the Mime

Received: Friday, December 1, 2006 4:35 PM

They deleted the whole Dirty Crabber myspace page because I uploaded some footage of Girls Gone Wild together with "Share My Banana". That's why your video isn't playing anymore. I made a friend request under Jeff Crabtree, and uploaded the video again in that video section. I don't know when or if they'll tag it for Mike Rembis.

Received: Friday, December 1, 2006 4:49 PM

You're quite a writer, Mike. Very interesting story. I understand most of what you said - cause I'm almost twice as old as you! You still used some words that I've heard in this modern age, but cannot comprehend.

Talk about slow computers - I'm supposed to get rid of some "Excess Files" - but I don't even know what they are! I'm not going to delete anything until I at least know what's in it!

Anyway - have a great Christmas and a wonderful New Year. God Bless to you and all of yours.

Victor

Received: Friday, December 1, 2006 5:05 PM
"Best" to you Mike! You definitely have a knack for writing. You remind me of "Andy Rooney". I think that's his name?????

Take care and Have a Happy Holiday!
MK

Received: Friday, December 1, 2006 5:26 PM
I was talking about the weather in Montana to a witch the other day.

She said, "yes, it is that cold!"
Walter Raine

Received: Friday, December 1, 2006 10:30 PM
Radio Shack still carries cassettes that clean VCRs. I know because I just called them this afternoon to ask!

Kathy McCormick

Received: Tuesday, December 5, 2006 9:11 PM
Ron Farnham wrote:

Happy Holidays. I have a tape player in my 2003 Cadillac DeVille. I make affirmations tapes and listen to them in my car. I still use cassettes. And DVD. I have been hooked on Johnny Cash for about two months now.

My Reply:
What the hell is an affirmation tape?

BTW, I am currently renting a 2007 Caddy, Pretty sweet. XM satellite radio and cd player but no cassette.

Mike

Ron's Reply:
An affirmation tape is a tape that you record things onto that

you want to happen. Say for instance you are struggling with a certain aspect of acting. Like for instance not remembering lines. You put on the tape something like this "You always remember your lines with great ease." Put it on there about ten times and listen to it. After listening to that over and over again your subconscious will believe that you easily learn your lines, and you will then do so.

Received: Monday, December 18, 2006 7:58 PM

I wanted to wish you a very merry christmas and a Happy New Year.

I am heading to Hawaii over the Christmas holiday!

Last minute trip. Going to Honolulu. Got a great baby sitting at the dog park for Lucy. I got lucky. Leaving Dec 20 coming back Dec 31.

Love ya

Susan

Volume X

Received: Monday, January 1, 2007 8:12 PM

Hey Mike, enjoyed your letter as usual. Not much happening here. Got exciting news for Christmas, we are gonna have another baby. I still talk to Debbie and Steve. Roger has been transferred or wanted to go to St. Augustine. The office is happy. Talk to Keiser every other week as well. Nobody is happy anymore. Except me. Here are a few pictures of me digging and some of my artifacts I have found in the last couple of weeks. I took a year off from digging. You'll like the last pic of my dogs in a "brokeback" moment. The kids are growing like weeds. If you want to make some money out there you should try to buy tax certificates or for the properties buy the tax liens. The banks do it with your money every year so why shouldn't you do it as well. Take care and give me a call some time.

Jeff

Received: Tuesday, January 2, 2007 7:43 PM
Happy New Year Mike. Attached is a song for you.
Ronald
Johnny Cash - I've Been Everywhere

Received: Wednesday, January 3, 2007 10:33 PM
Happy New Year Mikey!!!!!
Jill

Received: Tuesday, January 9, 2007 10:48 AM
hi mikey! you crack me up. thank you for the advice though. lol. my new years resolution is to focus on my acting and stay out of the local drama. don't hang out with people who really don't give a crap and most importantly not to forget to enjoy the journey....this short crazy thing called life.

please send me the name of your script to read on triggerstreet...i really would love to read it!

so to catch you up on me: (this is just for you and ellen by the way)

i am working on a local indie horror film now. i play an investigative photo journalist and am the heroine in the movie...kinda cool :) besides that, just got over my sickness thank God and am taking it easy this week.

i never told you but i played a wacked out senator for waste of space. when tom thompson asked me to do it i was really excited of course to get to play a crazy not too attractive character. lol.

i also did a music video with jon secada....you can go to his website or watch it on youtube. the song is called "free". the funny thing was the executive producers/ casting saw me in that crazy short where i played the slutty cowgirl and that's how they were initially interested in me. how funny is that. so it's true about never knowing who may see an indie that you did......i convinced vpf to get dave barrett to help shoot it....so they flew him in from l.a. to help with it. anyway, it was much fun and i actually love the song.

  other than that i just worked on an action/ adventure drama end of october, nov. dec. and am going back for some pick up shots and adr work the beginning of february. this one was thru my agent, great pay and will probably get distribution. that's about it for me. jim is busier than ever with his work....they are short handed and just hired 3 people that don't start for a couple of months. he does find the time to "race" and spend some time with me though :)

  say hello to ellen and give her a big hug from us! we miss you guys.
  sincerely your friend,
  Georgia

Volume XI

Received: Thursday, February 1, 2007 8:37 PM
They just keep getting better and better. I loved it!
From my wife, Ellen

Received: Thursday, February 1, 2007 11:17 PM
Hi Mike,
wow, I feel like I am in English literature all over again! Glad you are doing well. When I watch tv that promotes unknown stars..... I am expecting you at any moment. You are a trip.

  How is Ellen? Please tell her I said hello. Life is good here but Lowell's back surgery recovery has been tough.

  We have a neighbor that reads on the radio every AM and I think of you..she is 85 or something...keep on truckin'

  Take care.... alison

Received: Friday, February 2, 2007 3:48 AM
FYI if you Google Priscilla DuBas, you will get a ton of websites where her music and talents are reflected upon.

Farewell dear songstress, you are missed.

Corinne

Received: Friday, February 2, 2007 5:20 AM
mike i just read your latest email. it is 2 25 am CA time. I must say that while reading your email i went through many different emotions. all great, yet painful. please write a story about gambling and people, i feel that it would come out beautifully. the comment about your friend was sad and I am sorry. but do not let what was last sad by her and your comment disappear. it was truthful and real. i hope all is well for you. i would love to hear from you sometime.

chris

My Reply:
Thanks Chris, glad you liked it. I have a novel I am going to go back to later this year that deals with gambling. You drove that same stretch of interstate on your way out here. Hows the acting going?

Chris' Reply:
Busy, busy, busy. Filming, filming, and some more filming. Its going well. It's the beginning of my career I believe, very beautiful but somber at times.

I'm very thankful for everything that I have been given so far. How has life been for you of late? I will talk to you soon.

Chris

Received: Friday, February 2, 2007 5:36 AM
Hey Mike

Sorry for the loss of your friend. I'm actually listening to I'm a talking love right now and see has a great voice and is very talented. She will not be forgotten.

I was in St. Louis over the weekend for my Mom's 70th birthday and it was cold. I got a little taste of winter. 3 below with windchill and 6 degree and snow flurries when I left on Monday. Needless to say, I was glad to get home to Florida.

So I guess you have moved?

Keep warm.

Have a great day!

Susan

Received: Friday, February 2, 2007 10:50 AM

Still encourage you to write a column/ book or something. Your writing skills are exceptional!!!!!!!!!!!!!!!!!!!!!!!!!!! J Thanks for update!!!!!!

Received: Friday, February 2, 2007 8:18 PM

Mike, it's funny that Priscilla would e-mail that you need to write a book. I too think that every time you send us the e-mails. I enjoy reading them tremendously. Please keep me on your list and remember me when you're famous.

Pam Rush

My Reply:

Of course I would not forget you. Did you know Priscilla? I didn't realize that. I just saw the sun-setter awning commercial I auditioned for with Erica. I know you were there that day too. They should have picked us.

Mike

Pam's Reply:

No, I didn't know Priscilla. I too see the Sunsetter commercial. My acting coach got the job so I can't really complain. I don't go to Kathy's anymore. I only booked one job ever. It's just not worth the drive.
Pam Rush

Victor Helou was one of my vocal coaches who helped me develop my singing voice, a nice old gentleman, well over eighty years old when we first met. I kept him on the mailing list and he would write back periodically. I watched his memory fail more with each reply until he finally stopped writing back. I suppose he may have forgotten who I was.

Received: Saturday, February 3, 2007 7:35 PM
Mike;
Are you interested in Acting? I'm starting a new class on St. Pete Beach - next to the Don-Cesar Hotel. Mon - Wed- Fri - One Hour a day.
Let me know! God Bless,
Victor R. Helou

Received: Sunday, February 4, 2007 11:36 AM
HAiR closes today. I am glad it is over. Wish it could tour but I could not get anyone interested.
:(
corinne

Received: Thursday, February 8, 2007 1:07 AM
Cool man. I dig your writing. I am going to put your email address in the book I am writing. You are going to become a legend. People from all over the world are going to read your newsletter.
Ron Farnham

Volume XII

Received: Friday, March 2, 2007 10:09 PM
mike!!!!!!!!!!! hi, hope you and ellen are fantastic.....i really looked forward to this rr. it keeps me connected to you guys and that makes me happy. you are such a clever and entertaining writer!!! would somebody discover you already. gosh. when i make it mike, i'm getting you in somewhere damn it.

but i feel same as you...i need it now.....i can't just sit back and relax...there's so much to do, so little time. i feel time escaping me so quickly. it's not fair! the pressure to succeed, to keep busy because if i ever relax i feel like i'm slacking and i should be doing something to further my career! ugh!!!!! that's when the anxiety sometime sets in an then i have to say to myself just relax, your time is coming.

anyway, the best edit looks fabulous! marcos did a great job.....do you think he would be interested in re-editing the whole thing? maybe if we all chipped in to pay him? i think it would be worth it...i really feel that is one of the most important jobs in filmmaking (tv or movies) the editing! timing, reactions, flow....it's everything...the editor ultimately tells the story.

i'm done rambling....i'm going to eat something and go to bed. i have an early call time tomorrow.

say hello to ellen for me and hope to see you both soon!
ps i hope you win the competition mike!!!!!!!!
miss you guys!
hugs,
georgia

Received: Sunday, April 1, 2007 12:19 AM
From Ron Farnham
"One time, I ate my neighbors shit." ~Adam Sandler[12]

Volume XIII

Received: Monday, April 2, 2007 4:27 AM

well man it's been almost a year since we last saw each other. I am sure that we have both of things to share next time we meet again. I love the R.R., keep speaking your mind, it's all anybody really has. I hope the new town is better suited for you and life there is going well. Southern California is heaven, it really is. God has a condo in the Hollywood hills,

he's not as good looking as you would think. Life for me is pretty awesome right now. Learning who I am, really crazy shit man. Been painting a lot, writing poetry, auditioning, getting parts here and there.

Life as been good. I hang out in Venice beach a lot. I truly feel for the first time in a number of years that I am where I need to be. when you get some time man give me a call. take care man.

Chris

Received: Monday, April 2, 2007 9:55 AM

Well you can tell a story now you need to add the humor. Ha! I'm sure you've seen Hal Holbrook's one man show as Mark Twain. It's been years but I'd like to see it again.

LM

Volume XIV

Received: Tuesday, May 1, 2007 12:08 PM

You know, I've always had a philosophy about dreams. They come from your own brain so that alone oughta make it easier to figure them out. I think in your case you had an idea for a screenplay and it came to you at the exact moment you were sleeping. But if you really wanna crack this little mystery, you may wanna go to Google and find something under "dream analysis" D.D.

Received: Wednesday, May 2, 2007 4:40 PM
Your right Mike,
This was a good one.
I even made it... Cool, I'm an awesome dreamer!
Dave A. Barrett

Received: Monday, May 7, 2007 10:07 AM
Hey Mikey,

You are so funny! Check out Dreammoods.com for interpretation of your dreams.

Awesome job with the steve o' script man. I don't know how you come up with this shit, but you do!!!!!

Are you guys going to have a chance to come to LA. We found a house that I actually stayed in on one of my jaunts to LA. It has a backyard, guest room/office and a trailer attached for more sleeping comfort. Check out the pics I attached.

Hey I have a question for you, do you know copyright laws? I'm trying to copyright my superhero and I'm not sure how to go about it. I have the video that I submitted to the network and the paperwork, but I'm not sure if I signed my life away or not. My attorney said she could take a look at it and give me her advice, I just didn't know if you knew about this stuff.

Anyway, I hope you guys can make it out to LA. Tell Ellen I said HI and I miss you guys!!!!!!!!
Love ya!
Jill

Volume XV

Received: Saturday, June 2, 2007 7:21 PM
Mike & Ellen,
There is another year you have to add to that list. June 1, 1977. That is the day my daughter, Hilary was born in Dunedin. We had a 30th birthday dinner for her last night. Terry will be calling you guys with some news. Hope all is well with Mama Dog. We miss the girl. Hans

Received: Monday, June 4, 2007 9:51 AM
Hi Mike!
Thanks for the J. Really enjoy reading your words of wisdom! Nice Website! Take Care!
MK

Received: Saturday, June 9, 2007 9:28 PM
I want to see the new drivers license picture!!!! I laughed so hard about that. It was great talking to you guys last weekend. Miss ya!
Jilly

Volume XVI

Received: Monday, July 2, 2007 1:36 PM
Hi Mike,

As always your messages are great. I still strongly encourage you to do something with your writing TALENT!!!!!!!!!!!!!!!!!!!!

Start a column in the local newspaper???? Something! Your writing talent and descriptive abilities are to good not to pursue.

Food For Thought!

I am looking into "blogging" for the teens and a website. This might be something that would work for you. I don't know that much about it yet, but one site that might interest you would be Freewebs.com. Something to check out. Turns out Blogging started with journaling anyway.

Take care!
MK

Received: Monday, July 2, 2007 11:04 PM
Mike

I am now working with a hip hop artist as VP of his company. We have national and international distribution through Sumthing Distribution in New York. If you want to distribute a season of BEST, let me know and I can work out a possible distribution deal. If you think you can broker a deal for Whearty as well maybe we can get him distribute in a niche folk market. There are folk channels on satellite radio and in music stores. Let me know if you're interested. By the way, i have become pretty good friends with Jillian.

Ronald

Received: Tuesday, July 3, 2007 9:43 AM
Hi Mike,
I sure look forward to the Rembis Reports. You never disappoint me! Hi to Ellen and a pet for the animals.
Terry

Received: Tuesday, July 3, 2007 2:09 PM
Looks well preserved.
What else is up with you?
How are the sprinklers?
LOL
Corinne

Volume XVII

Received: Wednesday, August 1, 2007 3:05 AM
I really enjoyed this volume. You really had me involved with this adventure of yours. I am believer that there are no such things as coincidences or pre-destiny. Just that the universe sometimes may need you to do something very badly, for whatever reason none of us will ever know. I have been living things that have happened in dreams of mine lately. Very little or even subtle; i.e. having breakfast at a restaurant with a friend that I have never been to happened on Sunday, 7-29-07.
Weird time of life we our loving in, very fascinating though. Hope you are doing well and I look forward to hearing from you.
Chris

Received: Wednesday, August 1, 2007 8:00 AM
Best one yet, Mike. Either my heart was pounding or I was laughing my head off.

Still trying to decide how much was fact and how much was fiction. If all true, that string of coincidences really is creepy.

Miss you guys bunches. When do you leave on your trip? Hope you have a wonderful time!

Ellen, How are you and how are all the animals? How is little Einstein

doing these days? Wish you guys had never moved.
Terry

Received: Sunday, August 5, 2007 6:31 AM
How funny is that room and the mystery. Thank god you are alive. I thought it was going to get worse after you saw your feet.
HA HA!
j

Received: Monday, August 6, 2007 11:58 AM
I think you just had an experience that might make a good horror film. Though I'm not sure what the genre would be. Probably horror or noir.
D.D.

Received: Thursday, August 9, 2007 9:32 PM
oh Mike,
You need to get another hobby.
This is too long. Corinne

My Reply:
What do you mean too long? And I have lots of hobbies, writing this just takes an hour and a half a month. It's just spontaneous writing inspired by some recent event. Too long? It's not a movie, it's an essay. There are plenty of other essays out there that are a lot longer and say a lot less. I'm just trying to keep my friends entertained.
Mike

Corinne's Reply:
Sorry Mike, did not mean to offend you. It is just that I was on Vacation in NY and really just checking on business stuff.
I will read it, I love your musings.
Corinne

Received: Wednesday, October 24, 2007 12:09 AM
Wow, great story! Great writing. Really awesome, dude.
I've had many moments like that, when coincidences stack-up and get so intense - so wild - it becomes positively freaky.
It is scary, yet comforting when that happens - because it's a rare sign in this crazy world. It tells you: You are in the right place at the right time... This is where you are supposed to be... All the turns of your life, the good, the bad, the rushes and the pauses, the times you thought you were doing the wrong thing...they all led you to this moment of confirmation. You are on track.
How ironic that the alarm was set to the time of your birth because it sounds to me like the events of that night and next day represented an awakening, a realization, a 'birth' of new understanding.
I saw an Edgar Allen Poe quote recently: "All we see and all we seem is but a dream within a dream."[14]
Cb - Christian Badami

Volume XVIII

Received: Saturday, September 1, 2007 3:44 PM
Have a safe trip Mike. I will be on my way to LA on the 13th. Third time within a year's span.
Happy Birthday
Love to you both
Corinne

Volume XIX

Received: Thursday, October 4, 2007 11:43 AM
It was good, better than some of the others.
Unfortunately, I could not vote on it.
Corinne

Volume XX

Received: Thursday, November 1, 2007 9:44 PM
Happy 20th. Two more and you'll have enough for a 13-episode pilot season with an order for 9 back end episodes. Read the book by Ian Gurvitz titled *Hello, Lied the Agent*. You will love it. It talks about writing and pitching shows for TV.

Received:Friday, November 2, 2007 1:15 PM
Hey Mike,
Great report. Hope your trip was awesome! You'll have to share. Is the merry band of Yellow Bookers back to terrorize Billings yet? We'll have to catch up- preferably over strong drink.
What HAS happened to our youth? How dare they not go house to house and beg for candy on my favorite holiday! We only had 4 kids. Luckily I have not matured enough to stop dressing up. I was

1/2 of Siegfried and now mangled Roy. I make a slamming, yet disturbing, Siegfried. It was good to be a boldly tanned feline illusionist for a day. Plus I won an IPOD at work for my endeavors. :o

Hope you and Ellen are doing well.

Talk to you soon,

Allison Ohman

Received: Wednesday, November 7, 2007 3:04 PM
That's a great one dude. Keep sending.
And thanx for the plug!!
Cb

Volume XXI

Received: Sunday, December 2, 2007 10:57 AM
hey Mikey,

It's Kev your buddy.. How ya doin'? do you and ellen have Keedz yet??? lol

Nice report bout' Evel Kneivel. A friend of mine, Tony (a local film producer) went to Butte and took some footage of him...

Sorry to hear bout the Spidey fob (what is a Fob???)

Anyways Jessica tells me your livin' in Billings??? How that going for ya.. You travel a lot (lol)

I'm still here in Missoula and have had a tough time of it, but I love it, very cultural artsey, musical community.. I'm going to see "Tool" tomorrow at the Adams Center I have great seats just off the floor next to stage it should be a hellava show.. since never seem a Real Hard rock Concert (okay Pearl Jam) but they don't hold a candle to the Tool band.. Also created quite a web page on Myspace.. Do you have it for Drama? it's quite the networking tool for me.. I have had ova 3000 views and 900 people have signed my (frapp) map across the world..Yay

well send me an address so i can send you some pics, xmas card.. what eva..

here's the URL for my website
MySpace.com/kevlar420
also have music posted and 900 friends :>))
check it out.
peace
kev
_
k/p
a pig's orgasm last 30 minutes.
(In my next life I want to be a Pig)

Received: Sunday, December 2, 2007 11:25 AM

hey mike, i haven't talked to you in a long time! i just wanted to say that i always enjoy your Rembis reports. your sharp wit and light-hearted poignancy reminds me of one of my all-time favorite columnists, rick reilly from sports illustrated. so thank you for your thoughts!! it makes my day every time.

dang those squirrels are cute! you rock.

ciao, -scott

p.s. you might not want to get another spidey-head quite yet as you just gave every one of your friends a great gift idea for this christmas, and that would just add to the story of spidey-head III. but who will be the villain for the third installment? will the thief in the night emerge from the darkness yet again to rob you of yet another precious spidey-head? will the tumbleweed's mother, even bigger and badder than her son, come to avenge the merciless hit and run that took spidey-head II from you? sounds like a summer blockbuster to me...

My Reply:

Hi Scott,

I'm thinking Spidey might get replaced by Evel Knievel. How's that for a plot twist? I am so glad you like the R.R. Can you believe I actually did have 2, count 'em 2, lamos who asked me to stop sending it to them. So I did. They're erased. In the trash bin. No correspondence ever again, not even an "Okay, I'm cutting you off!" I just dumped them. Found it hard to believe too.

I also wanted to ask you if you had that footage I did for you, and if it looks any good, can I get a copy for my reel? I remember I played Jerry (because that's what I put on my resume) and I was shocked the Oscars people weren't standing outside your door when I was done. That was odd.

Let me know if you run across any screenplays that are Montana worthy, you know, could use Western scenery. I have got tons of awesome locations for the right script. Love to do some work.

See you later, Mike

Scott's Reply:

yes! i do have the footage, however there was a slight problem with, well- a lot of it.

you see, dan had an erection almost the entire time. a by product of the affection he was getting from his "fiancee," which, btw, was her first ever acting experience.

yup. strong like bull.

i can't remember at what time he became, uh, alert, but it might have been after you left... can't remember. i'll look into it... ah, to work with professionals...

Received: Sunday, December 2, 2007 1:50 PM
Hi Mike!

I loved this Rembis report. Thank you for always bringing a smile to my face and making me laugh out loud a few times! You are one of a kind and hold a special place in my heart :) It sounds like you are doing fantastic. I honestly can not wait for us to work together again....I say that with a definite conviction. On another note, I am so sorry to hear about Ellen's dad. Please give her our love and sympathies.

Update on me: I just shot a SAG national for Sea World...yay! I was so thrilled to book this one. It was a lot of fun. Look for it in January. I also did 2 political commercials and another one for Go to Meetings (this one should be pretty funny and will air on all the news stations like CNN, MSNBC, Fox News etc.) I typically don't like to toot my horn and tell people what I work on or have done...but I tend to tell the handful of people who I know will be truly happy and proud of me.

I miss you guys and truly hope we get to see you and Ellen soon. Greetings from Jim to you both.

Many hugs! Your BESTest friend,

Georgia

Received: Sunday, December 2, 2007 3:45 PM

Loved this report. Are you going to look for a Spidey 3?

I actually did meet Evel Knievel at a party in Feather Sound a couple years ago. He was rather egotistical but I figure he was entitled to be that way for a man who faced death for a living. I'm sure his body is glad to be resting now.

Trish

Received: Wednesday, December 5, 2007 2:26 PM

Hi Mike,

Great report. Also loved the slide show and video.

Hope all is well in Montana. We sure miss you guys.

Hello to Ellen and a pet for all the animals!

Terry & Hans

Received: Sunday, December 18, 2007 12:10 AM

Mike..

I really enjoyed reading the Rembis report.. keep em coming they are enjoyable to read.. you and your lady have a wonderful holiday...

Thomas LaRoque

Received: Monday, December 24, 2007 8:42 PM

Mike,

Funny you should mention heroes and superheroes. I recall being in Orlando having a conversation about the difference between a hero and a superhero. I think it's a combination of having powers, motivation to do good no matter what, and what you've done with it. If you don't have powers, then you're just a hero. But it also depends on how you got your powers. Spider-man has powers but he wasn't born with them and he's also mortal. So does that make him a hero or superhero?

I have an idea what it's like to be Spider-man because that was once my job. I actually got paid to dress like him and entertain at kids parties. I'm glad I don't do that anymore because it's not what I believe I should be doing career wise. I grew up with Spider-man too, but believe me, it's not the same as having to be him. I could tell you stories of all sorts about that.

D.D.

Received: Tuesday, January 22, 2007 5:56 PM

Holy shit...I just got to finally read this!!!!! Thanks for the x-mas card!!

We are bringing back my old tradition of Valentine's day cards instead.

I have your address in Livingston, MT.

Is this accurate?

Thanks for pushing the link for me!!!!

BESTest friend,

Jillian Kinsman- of course you guys can still call me jilly!!!!!

Miss you guys!

j

My Reply:

Hi Jilly,

No, that's wrong. Our address is in Billings MT and that's only going to be good for a couple more months because we just bought a new house in AUSTIN TEXAS! Yippee Kiyay! Seriously, we'll be moving here in the next 2 - 3 months and then our new address will be on Mumruffin Lane in Austin, TX.

How's that for a cool address? What is a Mumruffin? Not exactly sure how to describe it but I think Ellen might be one.

See you later, Mike

Jill's Reply:
Hey Mikey,
I didn't think it was correct. It usually rip off the addresses on the x-mas cards for changes, but I lost a few of them. I have both new addresses in my phone now.

Wow!!!! AUSTIN HUH!!! Congratulations!!! You will love it there. Not only is there film production, but the town is filled with YOUNG unpretentious people. I love Austin. We will be visiting often, especially when we'll be closer when we go back to LA. I am so sorry we never will get to visit you in Montana though. I have ALWAYS wanted to go there.

Anyway, expect a Valentine's day card from us at the Billings address.

A little update, we have decided to shoot Steve-O this summer, in FL. We are not going back to LA until the fall or beginning of next year. We still haven't finished with the script yet, but we have already started to scout locations. We are still aways away.

Anyway, that's it for now...have to go to Orlando today. I am starting some new acting classes, actually where Georgia and Darla went, Art's Sake.

Say hi to Ellen for me!!!!!
Hugs & Kisses to you both!
jilly

Volume XXII

Received: Wednesday, January 2, 2008 3:58 PM
Hi Mike,

Loved your report, as usual. Mama Dog doesn't look any too happy, however. That is quite the picture!

Happy New Year to you and Ellen. Of course your names came up yesterday when we were the guests of Andrew and Jacqueline for their annual New Year's Day get-together. We all still miss you and Ellen. We had bubbly and hors d'oeuvres at their house, and then once again went to Johnny's Italian Restaurant for a mid-afternoon lunch. Did you guys get to go there on New Year's Day before you moved?

Tonight we are having the coldest weather so far this winter. It is supposed to get down in the 30's. I suppose that would seem like a heat wave to you.

Hans is working long hours at Stock Yards Packing Company. One night he didn't get home until 11:00 p.m. The restaurants needed lots of meat right before Christmas and New Year's. Also, there are a lot of tourists here now.

Good luck, Ellen, in your up-coming job search. Please keep me posted on that.

Love,
Hans and Terry

Received: Thursday, January 3, 2008 10:53 PM

Once again, your Rembis report reminds me of a related story. Here goes.

Remember Elian Gonzales? The controversial Cuban kid? Well...a few years back when this was "hot news" I recall listening to the radio. These two shock jocks called a guy in Cuba who was a relative of Elian. It was mid February and he still had his xmas lights up.

They tried in vain to tell him to put away his lights. Every time they did this he responded angrily. Because it was in Spanish, they didn't know what he was saying, although they did understand one word which was "policia." Need I say more hombre? Feliz Navidad!

D.D.

Received: Saturday, January 5, 2008 11:58 AM
Mike,
You really didn't meet a Black Santa Claus did you? What is this world coming to? Got an email from Corrine with an invite thanks but too far to go. Christmas was quiet we went down to Mesquite NV did a little gambling had dinner more gambling, won a total of $30.00 which I gave back to them for my beer. Linda lost $150.00 which I was thrilled with she never knows when to quit. I think I will buy her the Kenny Rogers song "The gambler" and tell her to listen to the words.

So how is your planned move to Texas going?
Take Care
Sonny

Received: Wednesday, January 9, 2008 10:06 AM
Mama Dog looks like she parted all night.
Happy New Years!
Susan

Received: Wednesday, January 16, 2008 2:03 PM
Hi Mike,
Thanks for the fun Christmas letter! I have taken down the outdoor decorations, but still do have some indoors. These include a large "crystal" reindeer which I found at Walgreens. What's more, they assembled it for me!

As for Santa, I did meet him again this year! There is a man who attends my church who simply has to be the "real" one. When I mentioned it to him, he said that he had played the jolly old elf for many years in Illinois! This is my third real Santa sighting. Others occurred on a double-decker bus in London & in a bank in Hollywood!

Anyway, thanks again for the fun stories. We're finally getting winter weather in Florida now.

Cheers!
Kathy

Received: Tuesday, January 22, 2008 11:00 AM
Hey Mike,

My email address changed, and I don't want to miss the Rembis Reports.

Please change it in your contacts. Thanks so much.
Deanna

Volume XXIII

Received: Thursday, January 31, 2008 6:12 PM
Best wishes on your new adventure. Keep in touch!
MK

Received: Saturday, February 9, 2008 1:22 PM
Mike,

Hope your move is going well for you two. Let me know when you get settled in.

Sonny

Volume XXIII Addendum

Received: Friday, February 1, 2008 7:44 AM
Good luck in Austin. I've always wanted to go to Austin City Limits. I have a nephew that lives there. Did you transfer with YB?
LM

Received: Friday, February 1, 2008 1:52 PM
Thanks again for making me smile Best always!
MK

Volume XXIV

Bad news travels fast. Some friends wrote immediately upon notification of my sister's demise.

Received: Sunday, February 24, 2008 4:32 PM
Hey Mike ,
It's so sad what happened to your Sister... What a tragedy ...
Take care
Tommy

Received: Monday, March 3, 2008 8:50 AM
Hi Mike,
I got an e-mail from Sarah Dare about your sister's death. I am very sorry for your loss. I know nothing can be said to capture the sorrow that goes with it but I wanted you to know that I was thinking about and prayed for your family.
How is everyone else that was in the house?
Take care and God Bless,
Diane

Received: Friday, March 7, 2008 6:42 AM

I've been to Port Huron and Detroit many times. Reading your letter and looking at the pictures brought back many memories of living up north in neighborhoods like that. I lost a cousin in a fire who was like a sister to me. It was a tragic thing. How are your parents doing and how are you doing?

God Bless,
Lowell

Received: Friday, March 7, 2008 7:33 AM

Mike -- this is too good not to be published for the world to read! I wish you would send it to the New York Times or where??? If you publish this piece to the internet, somewhere in it use her full name Marian Rembis so your article can be found in a Google search. Many are googling "Marian Rembis" to keep abreast of what's going on. I would love to see 60 Minutes investigate the Kilpatrick corruption vis a vis city services situation, and I have sent an email to them. Should you decide to write also -- all suggestions and comments must be emailed -- email them at 60m@cbsnews.com .

I made a hard-copy of this for your mom, and as I handed it to her I said, "Read what Michael wrote -- it's a true memorial to Marian." She read it, said nothing, handed it back to me, and I said, "Keep it, that's for you." She turned away quickly. I thought I saw a tear.

Aunt B

Many other friends and relatives also encouraged me to publish this Volume.

Received: Friday, March 7, 2008 1:22 PM
Mike,

Thanks for adding me to your distribution list. I have not been to my mother's neighborhood since I was a teenager. Looking at the pictures, it seems surreal to me. Memories of Buscha's house with the beautiful garden and neatly painted porch steps are in my imagination. Inside it was very neat and clean; the small living room with the bedroom next to it, the large dining room, the small kitchen, etc. The neighborhood houses also were kept up.

It is so tragic about your sister and my heart breaks for you and your family.

If anything good can come from this, it is that I got to see you and your family again after all these years. I thoroughly enjoyed your write up and hope to stay in touch with you from now on.

Take care and God bless.

Your second-cousin (yes - who is really only 3 years older than you), Mary Ellen

Received: Friday, March 7, 2008 2:59 PM
Mike,
There are no words to express how sad I am for your loss. Please accept my condolences, and take care of your father and mother. They are going to need you.
Deanna

Received: Saturday, March 8, 2008 1:24 AM
Mike,
I'm sorry to hear about the tragic loss of your sister. I wish better times for you and your family.
- Jonathan Bergquist

Received: Saturday, March 8, 2008 9:02 AM
Mike:
I am so sorry for yours and your parents' loss. What a heart wrenching story. What a well written piece. I will pray for you and their recovery. Pam Rush

Received: Saturday, March 8, 2008 1:00 PM
Wishing you the best Mike as you get ready for a new adventure in Austin, Texas...
Looking forward to having lunch when you get back to Billings..
Tom LaRoque

Received: Saturday, March 8, 2008 7:57 PM
Mike,
I just wanted to let you know how sorry I am for your loss of your sister. I heard about it from friends in the old neighborhood....my heart goes out to you and your family. I am still trying to get in touch with Christine......if you would, please let her know she and her family are in our prayers.
With deepest Sympathy,
Gerri (Murawski) Norman

Received: Saturday, March 8, 2008 8:36 PM
Mike,
I am very sorry for your unnecessary lost. There should never be a lost like this the governments receives our tax dollars and do not use it wisely. I will keep your family in my prayers and you take care my friend.
Sonny

Sarah Dare forwarded this report to many others.

Received: Saturday, March 8, 2008 10:05 PM
I am sharing Mike's perspective (in writing on the fire that killed his sister and Detroit itself...(its not flattering).
Sarah

Received: Tuesday, March 11, 2008 8:05 PM
Hi Michael.
I'm sorry to hear of your sister's death. I liked the story about the plastic in the church.
The pictures.......
I'm sending some thoughts and prayers. Say Hi to Ellen.
Susan

Received: Wednesday, March 12, 2008 12:42 PM
nice write up Mike!....I'd like to be put on the list... Did your move go well? Gregory got arrested the other nite for shooting his bb gun at the romanians..they were throwing snowballs at his house....the police took him out in his bathrobe and slippers....otherwise they probably would of taken him bare naked!! last i heard he is in the hospital....that was on sunday.....let me know if you got this e-mail....oh yeah today is Mom's first day all alone since Marian's passed... her sisters went to the casino...I'm gonna call her in a lil bit to check in on her too......Later...Christine (*my other sister*)

Received: Monday, March 17, 2008 3:09 PM
Wow, Mike, that was tragic and inspirational at the same time. You should think about sending that to several places for publication!
-Matt

Volume XXV

Received: Friday, April 4, 2008 10:42 AM
I love the cat picture!!! When is the Cannes film festival?? we are going to Europe this summer before shooting to plan the wedding. Maybe we can do both and meet up with you to help!!!

Received: Friday, April 4, 2008 12:37 PM

Trust me on this: You will never stop roaming -- you are infected with Wanderlust. My father had it, too, to some degree, but under the circumstances of his life, he could wander only with the Travel channel and with me through the adventures I shared with him of my wanderings. And you are right, everyday comes with its own adventure, however, never to be repeated. Don't stop, don't ever stop.

Aunt B

Received: Friday, April 4, 2008 8:42 PM
Hello Mike

So you are now in Austin. Sounds good to me. And yes, I agree change is good. Living and see new places and things are great. I am still in Florida. Life is good. Still working at Yellowbook. It is still the same, but of course I like the people, customer, and reps.

Anyway, just thought I would say hello.
Good luck at the festival.
Susan

Received: Sunday, April 6, 2008 1:26 PM

Congrats on following your dream!!!!!!!!!!!!!!!!!!!!!!!!! You're right it doesn't seem like 2 years. I am still surviving doing POSH (Players of Safety Harbor) but the youth programs have priority so we are only doing one a year. The library currently is under construction to become bigger and better. We have finally found a venue to rehearse and perform at a place called the compass which is just down the street. A true blessing. Hopefully no more traveling company I hope. We are currently rehearsing "The Supporting Cast" by George Furth.

Best wishes on your forward step.
MK

Received: Sunday, April 6, 2008 5:09 PM
I will be sending this to a Venue member who has tons of miles, perhaps she will be willing to help.
But first. How many miles will you need?
Corinne

Received: Thursday, April 17, 2008 4:29 PM
Did you put more Dirty Crabber music in the re-edit? I thought you were going to send me a copy.
Thanks, Jeff Crabtree

My Reply:
Hi Jeff,
The only song we have in there is Share My Banana. Marcos, our editor, had so little time to do what he had to and meet the Banff deadline that placing more cuts would have required time he didn't have. He also did not use the whole song, which I am a little disappointed with, but I did give him total control to produce a cleaner edit. Hopefully, this will pay off. I am going to Cannes next month and will be pitching BEST to everyone I meet. If I get things the way I want them in the end, don't worry, I'll get more of your music in there. I'll send you a copy tomorrow.
Mike

Jeff's Reply: Thanks! Good luck at Cannes!

Volume XXVI

Received: Friday, May 2, 2008 6:01 AM
You are up late. Just wanted to say Hi. Good Luck with the auditions.
Susan

Received: Saturday, May 3, 2008 3:55 PM
I'm sorry, I'll take down the site asking for nude pictures of you...
Ken Power

Received: Friday, May 9, 2008 10:00 AM
Hey Mikey,
Finally just got to reading this. The reason why "Best" is placed everywhere is because you posted it on youtube. When somebody puts up a video advertising box from youtube and embeds it into their website, youtube has advertising "crawlers" look for key words just like google for advertisement purposes. If someone clicks on the video, Youtube and the advertiser of the website both make money. I do it in my links section of "Organic Reverence" I like the VO demo!!

Volume XXVII

After emailing this issue I realized that Yahoo had stopped letting me save the drafts and I thought the original was lost for good, so I sent out a harried email asking everyone to bounce it back so I would have a copy.

Received: Monday, June 2, 2008 7:35 AM
Mike;
I just woke up - and found this. Haven't read it yet - but you wanted it back, so here it is. Are you in the film industry? What

do you do? I don't remember that. Hope all is well. Take care, and God Bless!
Victor

Received: Monday, June 2, 2008 8:34 AM
garbage in garbage out!
LM

Received: Monday, June 2, 2008 11:35 AM
Congrats Mike!
-TT
Tom Thompson

Received: Tuesday, June 3, 2008 12:22 PM
Thanks again for the humor. Best Wishes
MK

Received: Thursday, June 5, 2008 6:33 PM
Wow!!! I cannot believe how much you are getting done. This is fabulous. I love both of the shorts you did at Cannes - they were great. I really enjoyed the twists that both of them had at the end. What fun.

There must be more going on where you live than there is here. I am amazed!!!

I always enjoy reading the Rembis Report. You are so open and interesting. You might even put all the musings together into a book at some point.
Deanna

Received: Friday, June 6, 2008 5:14 PM
Mikey,
I just watched everything....Congratulations!!! I am so proud of

you. You deserve it man!!! You must just be so proud of yourself as well. You work hard and you do a lot for everyone else. So it is really neat to see your success in Cannes. I updated the headline in my news sections on my website to highlight you and added the additional link to your youtube. Let me know if you want me to rewrite something. I'm trying to play catch up today, so gotta go.

Received: Wednesday, June 11, 2008 1:09 PM
Finally got around to reading the Rembis report... good to hear from you... Sorry I didn't have a whole lot of time to talk the other day. Take care and good luck in Austin...
Tom LaRoque

Received: Monday, June 23, 2008 8:53 PM
Hey Mike.
I sent you my script to read for feedback about two months ago. Did you ever get it? If not and you would like to read it, I can send it again.

IF YOU ARE THINKING ABOUT AUTO INSURANCE: DO NOT USE GEICO THEY WILL TAKE YOUR MONEY AND DO EVERYTHING THEY CAN NOT TO PAY ON A CLAIM. WANT TO KNOW MORE, EMAIL ME FOR DETAILS
Sincerely
Ronald Farnham
Cosmic Casting

Volume XXVIII

Received: Thursday, July 3, 2008 5:13 AM
Nice report Mike. Most of the time I don't have time to read it all even though your writing is excellent. But this one, I couldn't stop before the end :). I guess it reminds me of why I fell in love with Austin ...
Take good care.
Jonathan

Received: Thursday, July 3, 2008 9:23 AM
Hi Mike,
Still as talented as ever. Glad to hear that you are acting. Enjoyed your message. Again I will tell you that you write so well you should write a book or something?????
Hope this finds you doing well. Take care!
MK

Received: Thursday, July 3, 2008 3:59 PM
send away...I can't wait to see the new headshots!
Jilly

Received: Thursday, July 3, 2008 5:42 PM
Hi Mike
Just to say thanks, I've received the DVD now. And also thanks for the web link you sent me as well. Hope you are well and it seems that you are very busy! Am pleased with the double sugar film!
All the best
Ruth
really like your writing

Received: Thursday, July 8, 2008 7:02 AM
I got your message. I was on vacation all last week.
Yes, I still work for yellowbook.
Bye for now.
Susan

Received: Saturday, July 26, 2008 10:34 PM
Mike
I am going to be broadcasting on internet radio Party934.com as DJ Cocoa Beach Baby. I was thinking of reading your Rembis Report as part of my show or you can record a commentary and email it to me and I can play it on my show. Let me know.
 Sincerely
 Ronald Farnham

Volume XXIX

Received: Monday, August 4, 2008 6:12 AM
HI Mike!
Thanks for the update.
 Also thanks very much for the dvd which arrived. It's great! keep up all the fab work!!! you're doing great!!!!!! it we keep at what we want to do then we are doing what we want :)))
 all the best, Rebecca
 p.s. enjoy the weather - here we have torrential rain - UK august ;) !
 Rebecca Jameson

Received: Monday, August 4, 2008 9:18 AM
Mike,
Loved the email, it made me laugh. Glad to hear from you and

good luck with the acting. I love the new headshot. Not much going on here in Montgomery AL except HOT weather. The insurance business can only get so exciting – ha---so I love to read something that breaks up my day. BTW - I had a short experience in the movie business. I played an extra in the movie Big Fish. IT was filmed here in Montgomery. IT was fun – and if you look real fast you can actually see me in one of the basketball scenes. Well take care and keep in touch!

Vilma L Lawrence

Received: Monday, August 4, 2008 1:15 PM
Hi Mike,
Glad to hear that you are perusing your writing talents. Hope it works out for you!!!!
MK

Received: Monday, August 4, 2008 7:02 PM
I can't help but remember the scene in Reality Bites with Ethan Hawke and Winona Rider where she's been out there trying to find a job, any job, and is telling her mom this at dinner...her mom pipes up and says, "Well, times are tough Sugar-bugger, you're just going to have to swallow your pride. I know, I saw a commercial for Burger World and they had a little retarded boy runnin' the cash register. Now why wouldn't they hire you?" "Because I'm not retarded, Mom," Winona deadpans.

The next day they show her out at Burger World. Of course she doesn't last.

I remember when we were going through some transitions and I needed to pick up a second job. After looking and looking, answering ads for work but getting no where, it took a manager at McDonalds (yes Mickey D's) to basically tell me I was being too honest with my education and experience and that no one would hire me. No one would hire a college educated person with managerial experience for a JOB.

Those words reverberated in my head as I stood at his service counter in a visor and plastic name tag, the only one who spoke ENGLISH every day, morning after morning rush, pushing buttons and filling paper bags with greasy food.

Maureen

Received: Monday, August 4, 2008 10:56 PM
Good luck with all your new adventures.
Susan

Received: Sunday, August 10, 2008 8:42 AM
Really enjoyed the latest version of the Rembis Report...haven't had much time to even check my e-mail lately. Just finished up the Bozeman market and had a good one. I'm actually doing a little bit of work in Sheridan, WY for the company because they don't have any place for me to be until we launch Billings on August 25th...I hit my number in Bozeman but the team didn't hit the company goal so they all have to stay there while I get to sell in a new market with about 50K in existing revenue. About half of them hate me for it but too bad...they say it isn't fair...I say "fair" is where you take a pig to sell..

I'm glad to hear that the acting career is going good...I really miss having a lunch or two with you once in awhile...Sorry to say but I probably took about 15 to 18 customers from Yellowbook in Bozeman and I'll take another 20-30 in Billings...

Take care and talk to you soon.
Tom LaRoque
PS...I've been hosting a talk show on the Northern Broadcasting

Network one to two times a week. It is called Voices of Montana and it is a call in show based upon everything from state issues to politics. I was just told I'm probably going to be hosting it full time. It is an hour a day and I can still sell yellow pages. This means I'll be pulling in close to 100k by next year. so things are good that way.. take care..

Received: Friday, August 29, 2008 5:38 PM

Hey Pal just trying to get caught up in my emails. So you quit yellow pages? wanting to write for TV? want to act? Good for you I went the opposite way went to work and I hate it. I am slowly writing some humor but got stopped with the heart surgery and cancer scare, then I had to go to Sturgis for bike week. I found this report to be one of your best it had real feeling and insight to the corporate world we now live in. Or even the way society expects us to live go to work and kiss boss man's ass. The way I look at life is to say to hell with it I may not be here tomorrow so do it today. Mike I sent a photo of my bike it is my way of rebelling. I still have to call you about what I am writing about to get your insight on the idea.

Take Care
Sonny

Volume XXXII

Received: Sunday, November 2, 2008 2:43 AM
Hey Mike,

Glad to know you're alive and well. No, I haven't forgotten all about you. Believe it or not, I'm currently deployed to Kuwait. It came up very suddenly and I had to make a mad dash to get out the door to make it on time. I've been here since the beginning of September. I wasn't able to mail your materials back to you before

I departed. Sorry about that. I'll be back around February. If you need your stuff before then, let me know and I can have my wife ship them off to you.

We'll be moving sometime this summer. Not sure where to, though. Right now, the top 2 spots on our list are Florida and Texas (San Antonio area). So, who knows, our paths may cross again.

I just read your latest Rembis Report. Sounds like things are going really well for you. It's great that you've had so many encounters with people in the biz. Sounds like Austin is really a happening spot for film. If I make it to San Antonio, I'll only be 1 hr away. Maybe we can team up on a project or two. I'm really itching to do some work with more folks than just myself and my wife--not that the company is bad. Collaboration is a good thing.

Later, Stay well and keep in touch.

Marcos

Received: Sunday, November 2, 2008 2:54 AM
That question about the clown is as old as I am!
Thanks for the story :)
-Mr. Mike Note

Received: Sunday, November 2, 2008 9:36 AM
Hey Mike!

After reading that last report, I figured you'd appreciate these halloween pics. I partied on the 30th and 31st and the 1st of November. I managed to get 2nd and 3rd in two different costume contests. Btw the next time you see a movie and you don't understand something, it's probably because it was written specifically to mess with your head. You got burned big time by a clown for a long time and many others have gone down with you.

D.D.

Received: Friday, November 4, 2008 5:50 AM
Mikey,

You always crack me up!! How are you guys doing?? we have been so slammed here....i have had so much anxiety the last 2 days, I cannot sleep, hence the 5:30 am email.

BTW have you applied to put BEST onto IMDB? if so, are you having a hard time? I may know how to help you...the most important thing is outside links to Cannes Film festival and sometimes they want call sheets etc. Let me know if I can help you...I would like to get it posted...it will also help with Steve-O.

P.S. My friend Paul Morris is reading the script. Flynn had a lot of personal problems that we didn't want to burden him with......Anyway Paul is reading as we speak and will let us know if he can give us some input.

I got cast in a few films...check out my website for updates.....I went to New Orleans for a callback for a Lifetime Movie called Midnight Bayou....only 3 of us were up for the role...I found out last week that it was so close, but they went for the older looking gal. I was upset for a couple of days. I feel something good is going to come of it. The Fincannons, who casted it, called my agent and wanted to know everything about me. I auditioned for the director who was the Exec. Producer from the Witchblade series in the 80's. Ralph Hemecker. I love that show!!! So that was cool. Anyway, I keep plugging away and not trying to think about my losses you know what I mean?

Talk to you later and make sure you tell Ellen we said hello and it has been way too long since we talked...maybe we can chat over the weekend!

Big Hugs!!

j

My Reply:

Hi Jilly,

BEST definitely does not qualify for IMDB at this time. They sent me the rejection based on Cannes Film Market status, since that's not a contest, it doesn't count. I'm not going to try listing it there anymore, but I am following leads and making nice with some Hollywood TV people so I may get a pitch in some time this next year. We'll see.

I do hope Mr. Morris can help tighten up Steve-O the way you want it because I just don't have time to get back to it right now. I just finished stretching a short into a feature and couldn't get it past 78 pages unless I were to fill it with worthless fluff that didn't move the story along. In this case less was more, but the director wanted 90 pages and he still hasn't given me any feedback on it. I don't know what he's thinking now. I am also working on tightening up Great Falls. Since Ellen will be out of town next week, (she's going down to Harlingen for work) I will be able to really jam on that. Then I plan to finish the first draft of my Space Drama.

I just started a new acting class last night with Paula Russell and she is really cool. I'm involved in all kinds of productions on one level or another here, but I never seem to get any paying work. I'm glad you're getting enough recognition for some serious callbacks. You will book a role! A good one! I know it. Excited to watch Darla this week on LIFE. I've never seen that show. I know what it's like to be busy. I wish I had an assistant who could just submit things for me full time. In fact, I may look into getting one on O-desk.

Jill's Reply:

Hey Mikey,

Bummer about Best...that just sucks. Sorry.

Good luck with your writing, etc....You are amazing and Best and Steve-O really show it...I know my BESTest friends will be very successful!! Kudos to Darla...I have to look up when the show airs...do you know...maybe I can Tivo it?

Where is Ellen working and does she have to travel all the time for work??

Did your house sell in Montana? Are you guys doing well??

It sounds like you are really getting involved with a good acting community....I checked out the acting coaches' website...it looks good!! You'll get paying work...just keep hanging in there Mikey....it takes awhile to restart over in another city. I know you'll be successful!!

Miss you guys!! Big HUgS!!
jilly

Volume XXXIV

Received: Saturday, January 3, 2009 1:28 PM
Mike,
Happy New Year and Please be careful. Good luck with your film.
Sara Verner

Received: Saturday, January 3, 2009 6:02 PM
Hi Mike!
Happy New Year!

The R.R. is always entertaining and interesting. This issue, however, is the best. I liked how you carried the accident theme from a previous issue. In addition, the detail you shared of the accident research -- "how did it happen?" -- and the compassion you expressed for the young man that died was very touching.

All the best to you in your endeavors!
Vicki Wayne

Volume XXXV

Received: Friday, February 13, 2009 11:21 PM
Hi Mike,

Just wanted to let you know how moved I was by your letter...it was full of intriguing images and palpable emotions. I wish you and your wife all the best in your 'new' old home and hope you will stay in touch. One of my yoga students is moving to Tampa in April and wants me to visit and teach a workshop there in the near future, so who knows, Radames and I may see you again in the not so distant future.

Warm Regards,
Marsha Mann (Pera)

Footnotes

1 Article - Used by permission from AFP
2 Article - Used by permission from PARS International Corp.
3 Quote - Stanislaw J Lec
4 Quote - William Shakespeare
5 Article - Used by permission from Peter Birkenhead
6 Quote - Thomas Edison
7 Quote - Dr. Seuss
8 Quote - Dr. Martin Luther King, Jr.
9 Quote - Conrad Hilton
10 Article - Used by permission from Imagn Content Services
11 Quote - Calvin Coolidge
12 Quote - Adam Sandler
13 Quote - Edgar Allan Poe

Acknowledgements

PHOTOS

Black Santa Photo
Used by permission of Creative Commons License
Copyright © 2006 by AmericanBastard.

Mike Rembis Headshots
Used by permission of Valerie Tamburri.
Copyright © 2008

All other photography by Mike Rembis.
Billboard advertising image used by permission of Stockman Bank.
Copyright © 1987 - 2014

COVER ART

Original design by Michelle Ortiz.

ARTICLES

Tsunami-Orphaned Hippo Adopted by 100-Year Old Tortoise.
Copyright © 2005 by Agence France-Presse (AFP)
Used by permission from Copyright Clearance Center

Teacher loved music, singing.
Copyright © 2006 by The St. Petersburg Times
Used by permission from PARS International Corp.

Oprah's ugly secret.
Copyright © 2007 by Peter Birkenhead
Used by permission from Peter Birkenhead

Broken rigs, broken hearts collide in deadly blaze, Detroit fire shows impact of budget cuts on safety.
Copyright © 2008 by The Detroit Free Press
Used by permission from Imagn Content Services

QUOTES

1. Stanislaw J Lec, *"Unkempt Thoughts"* Poland (1909 - 1966)
2. William Shakespeare, *"Hamlet"* United Kingdom (1564 - 1616)
3. Thomas Edison, Accredited popular quote - Exact date and original context unknown United States (1847 - 1931)
4. Theodor Seuss Geisel (Dr. Seuss), *"How The Grinch Stole Christmas"* United States (1904 - 1991)
5. Reverend Dr. Martin Luther King, Jr., *Speech in Detroit, Michigan on June 23, 1963* United States (1929 - 1968)
6. Conrad Hilton, *Accredited popular quote - Exact date and original context unknown* United States (1887 - 1979)
7. Calvin Coolidge, *From his own memorial service program* United States (1872 - 1933)
8. Adam Sandler, *"The Buffoon and the Dean of Admissions"* United States (b. 1966)
9. Edgar Allan Poe, *"A Dream Within A Dream"* United States (1809 - 1849)

THE RESPONSE FILE

Special thanks to all of my friends, relatives, and cohorts who replied with such thoughtful prose and allowed me to include it in this edition.

My dear sweet wife Ellen Rembis, Maureen Smithorbob, Marsha Mann, Radames Pera, Vicki Wayne, Sara Verner, Jillian Kinsman, Dan Diaz, Marcos Baca, Michael Ferstenfeld, Tom LaRoque, Susan Tellmann, Mary Kay Smith, Vilma Lawrence, Rebecca James, Ronald Farnham, Richard Bohnet, Ruth Chan, Jonathan Rocher, Deanna Braunstein, Tom Thompson, Lowell & Alison Mather, Ken Power, Jeff Crabtree, Corinne Broskette, Barbara Brown Allen, Matt Parker, Christine Ball, Gerri Norman, Pamela Rush, Jonathan Bergquist, Mary Ellen Pierce, Diane LaFollette, Tom Rosinski, Sonny Baker, Georgia Chris, Adam ArNali, Scott Reus, Hans & Terry Knight, Trish Dempsey, Kevin Pierson, Christian Badami, Allison Ohman, Chris Pio, Edie Kobylka, Dave Barrett, Jeff Capron, Kathleen McCormick, Walter Raine, Missy Escribano, Annette Millan and especially our beloved Priscilla Dubas. You are missed and cherished.